Kilimanjaro Adventure

Kilimanjaro Adventure

One family's quest
to
reach the top
of
the African continent

Hal Streckert

Mission Press
San Diego

Kilimanjaro Adventure

Copyright© 1998 by Holger Streckert
All rights reserved.
No part of this book may be used or reproduced in any form or by any means, electronic or mechanical, including photocopying, without written permission from the author, except in the case of brief quotations in critical articles or reviews.
Printed in the United States of America.

All inquiries should be sent to:
Mission Press, P.O.Box 9586,
Rancho Santa Fe, CA 92067

Map by Tom Tamoria
Photographs by the author
Edited by Lynda Kennedy and Kathy Wittert
Cover Design by Stephanie Hall and Anja Ludewig

Library of Congress Cataloging-in-Publication Data
Streckert, Hal, 1955-
Kilimanjaro adventure: one family's quest to reach the top of the African continent / Hal Streckert.
p. cm.
Includes bibliographic references (p.) and index.
ISBN 0-9668123-5-2 (pbk.)
1. Mountaineering--Tanzania--Kilimanjaro, Mount.
2. Mountaineering expeditions--Tanzania--Kilimanjaro, Mount.
3. Kilimanjaro, Mount (Tanzania)--Description and travel.
4. Streckert, Hal 1955- . I. Title.
GV199.44.T342K557 1999
796.52'2'0967826--dc21   98-50574
                                     CIP

2 4 6 8 10 9 7 5 3 1

To Roko and Annie Bujas,
who introduced us to mountain climbing
and inspired us to tackle Kilimanjaro.

Contents

	Introduction	9
1	Kilimanjaro Summit	15
2	The Decision	19
3	The Mountain	41
4	Approaching the Mountain	51
5	On the Mountain	85
6	Getting Higher	107
7	Summit Day	133
8	Safari	167
	Appendix I Travel Information	195
	Appendix II Testimonials	205
	Appendix III Equipment List	223
	Appendix IV Measurements	227
	Acknowledgments	231
	Bibliography	233
	Index	235

Disclaimer

This book is designed to provide a narrative of our experiences in Africa. It is sold with the understanding that the publisher and author are not engaged in rendering advice in mountaineering. If mountaineering instruction is required, the services of a competent professional should be sought.

The activities depicted in this book carry significant risk of personal injury or death. Before you participate in any mountaineering activities, you are urged to learn as much as possible about climbing and seek qualified professional instruction or guidance. You must be knowledgeable about the risks involved and be willing to personally assume all responsibility associated with those risks.

This book is for entertainment purposes only. We make no representations about the accuracy, reliability, or completeness of the information or about the results to be obtained from using the information. The author and publisher shall have neither liability nor responsibility to any person or entity with respect to any loss or damage caused, or alleged to be caused, directly or indirectly by the information contained in this book. Political and social conditions are unpredictable and may add to the risk of traveling in Africa. The State Department maintains a "hot line" for Americans traveling overseas and should be consulted before travel.

If you do not wish to be bound by the above, you may return this book to the publisher for a full refund.

Introduction

For years, my wife and I had dreamed of going to Kilimanjaro and climbing it. Even as youngsters we had been fascinated by African adventures and the Great White Mountain. Before we knew what happened, we were in our early forties with a son, a middle-class grind, and a mortgage.

The daily routine kept us so busy that we didn't even have time to remember old dreams. Occasionally, there were glimmers of long-abandoned childhood fantasies.

Kilimanjaro radiates magic, which leaves people who see it for the first time speechless. There are many reasons, both rational and irrational, for this fascination with Kilimanjaro. The perpetual snow and ice on its peak seem contradictory to its location on the equator.

It is the highest mountain on the continent, surrounded by exotic places and people. It is a dormant volcano, and volcanoes are by definition fascinating and thrilling. And last, but not least, it is amazingly beautiful rising dramatically out of the plains and reaching into the sky, where the snow-covered peak blends in with the soft white clouds in an almost surreal setting.

Within the last decade, the Tanzanian Park Service has recognized the commercial value of Kilimanjaro and has been catering to the ever-increasing hordes of visitors. Climbing the mountain has become almost routine enough even for tourists with little or no climbing experience to attempt it. However, because of the severe altitude and the great distances from the various trailheads to the summit, there is no assurance of reaching the top — of "bagging" the mountain.

Although thousands of people attempt to climb the mountain every year, fewer than half succeed in reaching the crater rim and only a fraction of them reach the actual summit. Sir Edmund Hillary, the first person to summit Mt. Everest, was one of those who did not reach the summit of Kilimanjaro and a rescue team transported him off the mountain. Neil Armstrong, the first man on the moon, also made an unsuccessful attempt. Both of these modern-day heroes are capable of superhuman accomplishments, but the summit of Kilimanjaro eluded them.

The idea of climbing Kilimanjaro with my wife, Diane, and our son, Kyle, was rekindled seemingly out of nowhere. However, even with modern equipment, guides, porters, and all the conveniences established on the mountain, it still takes a tremendous physical effort to reach the summit high in the thin atmosphere.

For the great majority of people, this is one of the most physically demanding experiences of their lives. That certainly was true for us collectively as a family, but we wanted a shot at it. At the time of this trip, our son was a typical seventeen-year-old, which added the challenge of dealing with the teenage mentality in a third-world country. We did not know what to expect from that combination.

Why did we decide to climb Kilimanjaro, which is a physically demanding, high-risk undertaking, instead of a more normal trip for a family to say, Disney World? Of course, there is no simple answer.

We enjoy mountain climbing, but most of our experiences had been in the local mountains in California and some peaks in the Swiss Alps and Mexico. Therefore, the time was right to tackle a big one and make a real adventure out of it. There seemed no better place to start than with the highest mountain on the African continent.

The more usual family destinations are enjoyable, but there is no risk and no reward, and, therefore, they have a distinct feeling of banality. However, with mountaineering, the bigger the mountain, or the riskier the ascent, the more challenging and rewarding the experience. And finally there was the spirit of adventure: the long trip, the exotic places, meeting people of different cultures, the unknowns and uncertainties of the mountain, and the wild animals.

It was not just the physical challenge and the beauty of the mountain that attracted us to Africa, but the opportunity to experience this adventure as a family. This would add a whole new dimension to climbing the mountain and simultaneously to the spirit of our family. Could three people of vastly different interests, physical and mental capabilities, separated by a generation, have a positive experience trekking to a small summit plateau in a remote corner of the world?

We had no clue how to start organizing an expedition to Kilimanjaro. So, of course, we simply got on the Internet and located an adventure-travel company that specializes in Kilimanjaro and East Africa. That part was easy, but international travel to the depths of Africa has some unusual requirements, such as medication and vaccinations, and because of the political and social instability, there were some concerns for personal safety. We therefore contacted previous clients of the adventure-travel company and many responded with quite lengthy messages.

The response was overwhelmingly positive, which reinforced our conviction that this was a worthwhile endeavor. One comment in particular reflects the flavor of the messages we received: "... climbing Kilimanjaro and touring the Kenyan National Parks are world class experiences that you will never forget." In retrospect, we could not agree more. We became so charged up after the trip that we had extra vigor in our daily lives and an extra boost of self-confidence.

Family, friends, and acquaintances were eager to hear about our experiences and we were more than happy to share them. Two local reporters got wind of our trip and they promptly interviewed us and published articles in their newspapers. This kind of media attention was a new experience for us.

This book is the real account of our adventure to Kenya and Tanzania, our attempt to climb Kilimanjaro, and to stand on the highest summit on the African continent together as a family. When we first started this adventure, I thought it was about climbing the highest mountain on the African continent. By the time it was over, I knew there was more to it than that.

Of course, a trip to Africa would not be complete without a photo safari to one of the game parks. The safari to the Masai Mara National Game Park was not a continuation of the physical challenge provided by the mountain climb, but a pleasant way to complete the African adventure. We experienced first hand the wild and exotic animals, normally seen at zoos or on television. There is nothing like it in our well-regulated, safety conscious, industrial world.

To come face to face with giant herds of zebras and wildebeest, and with gazelles, monkeys, giraffes, and elephants is nothing short of spectacular. Full-grown lions roaming freely in the tall grass and feeding on a fresh kill is a sight to behold. We observed a rare leopard up close and a nervous cheetah mother with her two little cubs.

While we were walking on the bank of the Mara River, a giant river hippopotamus attacked us, and we ran for our lives. The excitement and sense of adventure was as real as it gets. We had the opportunity to meet and speak to real Masai warriors. These are fascinating people with a completely different outlook on life than we are used to.

Our daily lives are normally filled with attention to our careers, routine, chores, and some valuable and seemingly diminishing leisure time. In this age of computers, television, and the Internet, we tend to expect to be entertained — to have Hollywood generate a sense of excitement.

The entertainment industry does a fantastic job, but they can only do so much to imitate adventure. And it will always remain just that, an imitation. To get the real effect, you need all the elements of adventure, including travel to exotic places, uncertainty, challenge, risk and reward, and more than anything to experience it first hand.

Hopefully, this account of climbing Kilimanjaro will fascinate both aspiring and experienced mountaineers and will inspire other families and groups to consider this type of adventure as a truly enriching experience.

1

Kilimanjaro Summit

It was shortly after midnight and freezing cold in the stone hut when our guide, Fred, yanked us from our peaceful slumber. By the time Diane, Kyle, and I got dressed and forced down some breakfast, most of the other climbers were already ascending the steep slope toward the crater rim. We rushed onto the trail, which was lit up by bright moonlight. We set a steady pace and in short order passed the other groups of climbers and progressed to the front of the line.

The trail meandered up the barren, steep face of the crater pyramid. Our hiking boots dug into firm ground until we traversed the notorious switchbacks above the Hans Meyer cave. There we encountered wide swatches of loose sand and scree, and we would slip and slide down more than we proceeded up. It seemed like we were taking two steps forward and three back. It was a breath-robbing way to climb in the thin air and the darkness of the night.

My lungs were pumping like a two-stroke engine trying to suck in enough air to supply my tired muscles with much needed oxygen. The immense scree field kept punishing us and did not seem to want to end.

We had been climbing for several hours and feeling the effects of the steep slope and the rarefied atmosphere. Diane was behind me and I overheard her asking Fred, "Is this scree field ever going to end, or does it go on forever?" He chuckled, "You doing great. Not too much longer." Then she fell back into an almost trance-like state and continued to thrust one foot in front of the other.

Plodding along in the still of the night, I was in a similar trance, concentrating on taking one step at a time. In this state of mind it occurred to me that living in the city, with cushy office jobs, we spend a great deal of time and effort keeping our bodies in a narrow "comfort zone."

We let our bodies dictate to us. We eat when we're hungry. We go to sleep when we're tired. We have coffee to keep us awake. We don't let the climate control in our cars or houses vary more than a few degrees from a pre-set temperature.

All this is different in the mountains. When you go high in the mountains, it becomes obvious that your body doesn't want to be there. The higher you go, the more it rebels. The air is too thin to breathe and supply the muscles with enough oxygen for proper movement. The food tastes bad and is difficult to digest. Headaches and light-headedness develop from lack of oxygen. The symptoms get worse with altitude, including leakage of fluids into the lungs and swelling of the brain.

If you listened to your body, you'd never go higher. But the mind forces the body to continue. It's almost pure willpower that gets you to the tops of big mountains. It is definitely mind over

Kilimanjaro Adventure 17

matter. You have to push your body out of the comfort zone and force it to cooperate, even if it hurts and tells you to stop. The mountain thrusts out a challenge and it's extremely satisfying to accept it and to win.

The angle of ascent increased to a debilitating forty degrees, and the ground was as loose and slippery as a big pile of ice cubes. The trail snaked through a field of massive boulders, which occasionally rocket down the crater pyramid, smashing anything and anybody in their path.

Kyle was becoming exhausted. His legs were starting to feel wobbly and it became hard for him to stand, much less climb up the slippery scree. He looked ahead and saw me slip on the loose scree and slide into the volcanic sand.

I had no trouble catching my balance, but Kyle glanced down the mountain. Even in the moonlight, he could tell that the slope quickly dropped away. It was a scary thought and he felt a slight faintness imagining a fall down the steep slope. He decided it was better not to look down.

I noticed that he set his sights on climbing up and ignored the negative thoughts of tumbling down the mountain. Then he wondered out loud, "If we don't reach the crater rim soon, I won't be able to go much further."

And after what seemed like too many hours, we fought the last difficult steps up the infamous scree field and, suddenly, we were standing on the crater rim of the dormant volcano. In front of us was a large plateau covered with ice and snow that shimmered in the bright moonlight.

We gazed in awe at the snows of Kilimanjaro, made famous by Ernest Hemingway in his gripping short story. It was a beautiful winter wonderland, not on the North Pole, but on the equator.

We continued hiking along the exposed crater rim, desperately trying to suck enough air into our freezing lungs to propel our tired legs upward to the summit. The wind was ripping across the rocky terrain causing a ferocious wind chill and I had to bury my face deep inside the hood of my jacket.

Kyle, exhausted, was relieved to be on level ground. He quickly got a second wind and was able to continue at a strong pace. "Be careful that you don't burn out before we reach the summit," I warned. He pretended not to hear me.

We skirted past tall glaciers, which made their presence known with eerie creaking and groaning noises. The trail was mostly clear of snow and ice due to the volcanic heat conducted through vents from deep within the interior of the earth. The trail was clear until we walked into a field of sharp, wind-swept pinnacles of ice, which resembled giant inverted shark's teeth. They were waist high and shattered as we plodded through them in our rigid hiking boots.

The air was so devoid of oxygen that we had to stop again and again to take five or six deep breaths before continuing. We had trained hard and traveled halfway around the world to get to this mountain. We had been hiking and climbing for over four days. Now we were finally approaching the ultimate goal of this long, arduous trek — the summit of Kilimanjaro.

2

The Decision

Early in the year, we discussed the possibility of a family trip during the summer. The intent was for it to be fun and exciting for all of us. We kicked a few ideas around, but at the time, we could not come to a consensus. Although our daily lives kept us busy, Diane and I frequently went to the mountains on weekends for day hikes, to get away from the daily grind and the city, and to enjoy the outdoors.

In April, we went hiking in the Grand Canyon along the Kaibab and Bright Angel trails. The evening before our hike we checked out the trailhead and the conditions on the upper part of the trail. The first few switchbacks were clear, but then a thin veneer of ice covered large sections of the trail.

The sheets of ice created a surface as slippery as freshly waxed parquet and we considered using crampons. Crampons are a pair of steel grids with sharp spikes that attach to the sole of the boots to grip into ice. We figured that the icy conditions existed only on the upper switchbacks, and we could traverse those easily without crampons.

Once the sun dipped below the horizon, the spectacular display put on by the Hale-Bopp comet smeared across the northwest quadrant of the celestial sphere dominated the night sky. Of course, we had already watched it at home in San Diego, but it was more vivid and detailed here, away from city lights. We retreated to our room for a good night's rest, in preparation for an early start down the canyon the next morning.

The south rim would become infested with tourists as the day progressed. But due to our 6:00 A.M. start, we had the trail completely to ourselves. We plodded down the well-groomed path in the half darkness of the early morning, being extra careful on the slippery ice.

It turned out we made the correct assessment with the ice and it lasted for only a short way down the trail. We watched in awe the sunrise from within the depth of the canyon. The colors painted onto the orange sandstone walls were as brilliant as a laser show.

By the time we approached the Indian Garden Camp, we encountered several hikers who had spent the night in the Canyon and were on their way out. At Indian Garden Camp we refilled our water bottles and continued on our merry way, passing hikers who were descending toward the river from the campgrounds.

By now, we were deep within the Canyon although we had the impression that we were actually in the mountains. We were surrounded by steep walls and towering peaks reminiscent of the Andes in Patagonia.

We rounded a sharp bend of the trail and were confronted with terrain shaped like a giant bowl. The trail snaked along the walls of the bowl and once we reached the bottom, it was just a few more minutes and we could distinctly hear the fast flowing Colorado River. We made it from the south rim to the murky river in two and a half hours.

The sun was warming the cool air trapped in the tight sandstone valleys. We changed to lightweight shorts on the banks of the river. We had a quick bite to eat, washed our hands in the river, and turned around for the hard part of the hike — back up to the rim.

Unlike climbing in the mountains, the uphill effort of the hike comes after the downhill part. The temperature was perfect, not too hot, not too cold, and we set a good pace. We bumped into several hikers we had passed going down.

They said, "Looks like you had enough and decided to turn around early?" "No, we had a quick snack at the river and are on our way back up," I replied. "No way, you couldn't have gotten that far ahead of us," they countered. "I guess time flies when you're having fun. You'll find our initials scrawled in the wet sand of the river bank." That convinced them.

The hike up went even better than down in terms of making steady progress. We reached the rim in three and a half hours. It was only 1:30 P.M. and I felt good enough to go back down again. Sarcastically, the signs along the trail warn against doing the round-trip even once. I wanted to do it again right then. Diane was too tired and her feet rebelled, so I did not insist. I was still charged up though and my mind was racing trying to figure out what to do next.

As a teenager, I had dreamed of Africa and spending time there, but I had long since abandoned my boyhood fantasy of African adventures. I am still fascinated by exotic animals in zoos, books, and on television. Combining my interests in the mountains and wild animals gave me the extravagant idea of going to Africa and climbing Kilimanjaro. And to top it off, Kilimanjaro is the highest mountain on the African continent and is one of the seven summits*.

"Okay, so you don't want to do the Canyon twice in one day. How about climbing Kilimanjaro, followed by a safari," I said to Diane. "Sure, sounds great," she uttered in disbelief. "No, I'm serious, why don't we go climb Kilimanjaro later this year?" I explained, looking her straight in the eyes.

She pondered the question briefly, realizing I was dead serious and added excitedly, "I'm game. I've always wondered about Kilimanjaro, and with training I think I could do it." With that the ball got rolling, and all we had to do was figure out how our son, Kyle, would fit into the plans.

What were our qualifications for attempting something as difficult as climbing Kilimanjaro? Our own climbing experiences did not include a major, world-class mountain. Our interest in mountaineering started about ten years ago when a couple of good friends of ours, Roko and Annie Bujas, invited Diane and me to scale Mount Whitney with them one weekend.

Mount Whitney is the highest mountain in the contiguous United States. We were in reasonable shape and it sounded like a great way to spend a weekend. Especially, because we didn't know what to expect. We drove to Lone Pine, a small community at the foot of the mountain, where we spent the night.

---

*The seven summits refers to the highest peak on each of the world's continents and consists of: Everest, Asia (8848 meters), Aconcagua, South America (6959 meters); McKinley, North America (6195 meters); Kilimanjaro, Africa (5895 meters); Elbrus, Europe (5642 meters); Vinson Massif, Antarctica (5140 meters); Kosciusko, Australia (2229 meters).

Kilimanjaro Adventure

Our ascent began at the trailhead at Whitney Portal with heavy packs on our backs, loaded with tents, sleeping gear, cooking utensils, and food. It was slow going at the lower altitudes but very enjoyable to be on a good-sized mountain. We spent the first night at the Trail Camp at 3670 meters. This was our first experience of any kind with altitude, and we started feeling the first signs of altitude sickness, including light-headedness and poor appetite.

The next morning we strapped on a small daypack and marched to the summit in our sneakers. Our shoes were just one indication that we were rookies. Overall, we had luck with the weather and conditions on the mountain. It was thrilling to reach the summit, especially when numerous, more experienced "mountain men" had to turn back due to fatigue.

Since that first experience on Whitney we enjoyed the freedom of the hills, and frequently climbed the mountains in the greater southern California area, including Mount Baldy, San Jacinto, San Gorgonio, and Whitney. A few years after our first Whitney ascent, I went back with Kyle when he was thirteen.

The two of us climbed to the summit of Whitney from Whitney Portal in less than six hours, and completed the round trip in less than twelve hours. This would be remarkable for an adult in reasonably good shape and demonstrated the mental and physical toughness he was capable of.

A few years later, Diane and I returned and repeated the feat. We have also climbed in the German and Swiss Alps, and in Mexico, and ascended well over one hundred peaks. Some of the enjoyment in climbing comes from the self-reliance, the challenge, and the beautiful scenery, but also the camaraderie and the friendships that develop with other climbers. To top it off, it's a great way to stay in shape.

The highest mountain we had climbed before Kilimanjaro

was Popocatepetl, an active volcano outside of Mexico City, with a height of 5452 meters. Popo is a beautiful, symmetrical, cone-shaped volcano with a permanent ice crown surrounding its fire-breathing crater.

We made our climb in late 1993. Just a few months later, the volcano erupted and started spewing out huge billows of volcanic ash and flaming rocks high into the atmosphere. Nearby towns had to be evacuated, and there was talk about how to protect Mexico City if the eruption got any bigger. The current eruption has lasted for several years and, needless to say, has resulted in the closure of Popo to climbing.

We flew to Mexico City and drove to Tlamaca where we spent the night in a very comfortable climber's hut. The next morning we got an early start and proceeded up the mountain with headlamps. We reached the ice field at daybreak and strapped on our crampons. The approach was straightforward: just head up the ice. It felt like we were trying to walk up one of those Olympic ski jump ramps.

We fought our way up the steep, crevasse-free ice. After a seemingly endless mountain of ice, we finally reached a narrow strip of volcanic sand surrounding the deep crater. At the lower crater rim, we were greeted by a sight straight out of *Dante's Inferno*. When Dante and his companion, Virgil, enter through the gate of hell and find themselves in the vestibule of hell, he describes it with these words:

"Where a great cliff fell sheer, its beetling brow
Ringed with huge jagged rocks, we reached the brink
Overhanging the still ghastlier dens below;

And here so overpowering was the stink

> *The deep Abyss threw off, that we withdrew*
> *Staggered, and for a screen were forced to shrink...*
>
> *...Plumb in the middle of the dreadful cone*
> *There yawns a well, exceedingly deep and wide,*
> *Whose form and fashion shall be told anon..."*

We felt like the legendary explorers, Dante and Virgil, as we gazed down into the bottomless chasm. The live volcano was complete with smoke, ash, and sulfur gases that stunk like rotten eggs, and robbed us of valuable oxygen. Nonetheless, we continued to the summit at the far side of the crater.

The sky was clear and brilliant except for an occasional plume of sulfur-containing breath from the volcano. We got a fabulous view of neighboring Iztaccihuatl and Pico de Orizaba in the distance. A thick layer of smog blanketed Mexico City to the west of us. We descended around the crater rim and proceeded down the steep glacier. Then disaster struck.

My crampon points sheared out of the treacherous ice on the upper part of the ice field. I fell, slammed face first into the ice, feeling like I had been hit with a baseball bat. Sharp shards of ice exploded in my face, stinging my skin. The painful impact left me dazed. I was unable to drive the pick of my ax into the ice with any authority, and I careened down the bumpy slope flat on my belly.

Due to the steep forty-degree angle, I picked up blinding speed and found myself partially airborne. The short bursts of flight were rudely interrupted by punishing bounces off the steel-hard glacial ice. My crampons grabbed the ice and violently windmilled me head over heals as though I was a doll. The multiple blows and crashes took their toll, knocked me unconscious, and sealed my fate.

It was the most devastating slide a climber could imagine, and it seemed as though it would never end. At last, the slippery ice receded about 500 meters later. A mortal distance greater than the height of the Empire State Building. All downhill — on rough, jagged ice!

The ice was followed by black, volcanic scree, dotted with rocks and boulders previously ejected by the angry volcano. My mangled body, looking more like a bloody rag doll than a human being, miraculously missed the vicious boulders randomly poking through the serrated ice. Hitting any one of them would have been fatal.

I finally came to an abrupt stop in a bunker of scree. This made for a somewhat "cushioned" landing, but the fine scree particles became permanently embedded in the hundreds of cuts I had suffered on my head, face, hands, and legs.

I was bleeding profusely, especially from my face, mouth, and hands. My jacket and pants were ripped to shreds. My ice ax had been launched early in the fall, while I was desperately trying to self-arrest the downhill slide against gravity.

The final landing pad was near an outcrop called "Las Cruces," Spanish for the crosses. It is a small cemetery marked with several metal crosses, memorializing prior fatalities on the mountain. I had almost joined them — permanently. But that day I had a guardian angel looking over my shoulder.

Diane was descending with me at the time. Fortunately, we were not roped together, or I might have pulled her down with me. However, she had the horrifying experience of watching me take the quick way down.

If my attention hadn't been selfishly focused on my own precarious situation I would have felt sorry for her. Word of my fall quickly spread on the mountain. My wife and friends, Roko and Annie, were descending, but took over an hour to reach my crumpled body. A group of experienced alpine mountaineers from Germany, led by a professional mountain guide named Johann Vollmayr was nearby, and immediately came to my rescue. I am indebted to each and everyone of them who selflessly assisted in getting me off the mountain alive.

I was severely cut, bruised, and banged up with a relentless concussion, but miraculously had no broken bones. The cuts and bruises healed quickly; however, the worst damage was to my ankles, which had been compressed when my crampons were driven into the ice during the slide.

After much pain, physical therapy, and hard work, my ankles took about two years to heal. You would think that such a cruel fall would knock some sense into me, but that was not the case. Once my ankles started to heal, Diane and I went for short hikes in the local mountains. As they improved, the hikes got longer and we tackled bigger and higher mountains again.

One year, we flew to Germany to visit my parents, and we announced, "We've come over to Europe to do some sightseeing in Switzerland and to climb the Matterhorn." "We know Frau Perren, who owns the Haus Solvay in Zermatt," they said immediately. "We'll call and see if we can all stay." Sure enough, there was room for the time slot of interest and we all headed south.

We arrived in Zermatt to witness a sleepy village situated at the foot of the Matterhorn in one of the most beautiful valleys in the world. The cool air wafting between the luxurious chalets was faintly scented by the bouquets of blooming flowers decorating the ornate balconies. The town is so quaint and snug that cars are not only unncessary but also banned.

We could see the Matterhorn jutting aggressively into the blue sky from our bedroom window. Some days it had a white cloud streaming from the vertical, triangular wall near the top, due to the pressure drop as the wind roared around the granite block. It looked a lot like the plume cloud that boils off Everest in the leeward jetstream.

Unfortunately, a late winter snowstorm had just hit the mountain, making it impassable except to the most experienced and daring climbers. We don't consider ourselves to be in that category. We thought we would attempt nearby Monte Rosa instead, but again the weather didn't cooperate.

When all else failed, Kyle and I climbed the Breithorn, a 4165-meter neighbor of the Matterhorn. The Breithorn is one giant pile of hard-frozen snow with two broad peaks, so we strapped on our crampons and marched to the top. The only really exciting part of the climb was crossing over from one peak to the next, along a narrow ridge with steep, icy slopes on either side.

Now it was time for us to check out the conditions on the Matterhorn. Diane, Kyle, my father, and I all hiked to the Hornlihutte, a luxurious hiker's facility part way up the mountain, with a restaurant and overnight facilities. It is supplied by helicopters on a daily basis in the summer.

I continued solo up the trail until the conditions became so treacherous that I decided to wait for the next trip to Switzerland. However, over the next few years, Kyle developed other interests and, like a typical teenager, spent less and less time with his parents.

For several years, Diane and I had kicked the idea around of going on a trip to Africa, to climb Kilimanjaro, and to go on safari. We'd get excited just talking about it and knew that some-

Kilimanjaro Adventure

day we would go. We had to work out all the practical considerations, including one major concern — Kyle. Should he go and under what circumstances?

When we asked him about Kilimanjaro at age fifteen he was not interested, and it would not have been enjoyable to take a reluctant teenager. Diane was disappointed about his attitude toward the trip and couldn't understand why he would not jump at the opportunity to travel to Africa.

She explained to him, "When I was growing up airline travel out of the country was considered an expensive luxury. I would have been ecstatic if my parents had planned a family trip to Africa or some other exotic location." With typical teenage sarcasm Kyle responded, "I know, I know. And you had to walk half an hour through the snow to get to school."

It seems times have changed and the lure of far away places might have diminished among our kids. For Kyle, going to Africa was not much different than from going snowboarding in Utah. Both Diane and I would miss him and feel bad excluding him from a once in a lifetime chance to experience Kilimanjaro and Africa.

We shelved the idea until Kyle was a little older, since we wanted him to be able to participate. After the hike in the Grand Canyon, Diane asked Kyle, who had just turned seventeen, "How about going to Africa and climbing Kilimanjaro later this year? Would you be interested in going with us?"

"Well, I'm not crazy about the idea, but let me think about it," was his first response. The mountain didn't intimidate him, but the idea of spending time with his parents was not high on his list of fun things to do.

After we discussed the matter and brought it up several times, he warmed up to the idea. Part of it was because he knew

Diane really wanted him to be with us and he didn't want to disappoint his mother. He liked the mountains, but never seemed to find the time for them while we were close to home. However, he was starting to understand the significance of the entire undertaking and the unique opportunity.

He told us that while he was thinking about it, he would mention it to some of his friends, and it surprised him how excited they got about the prospect. We think that convinced him. Whatever it was, we were happy that he was coming around. We were still debating what to do, when Kyle made it clear that he would be interested in going along. By then, it was well into the year and we had to make plans quickly.

Where do you start when you want to go to Africa and climb Kilimanjaro? This is the second half of the nineties, so you start on the Internet, of course. I pulled up Yahoo on the computer, typed in Kilimanjaro, and pressed search.

A moment later there were eighteen hits. Great. I scanned them, and three in particular were of interest, because they were commercial outfits specializing in organizing climbs and safaris. I clicked on them and sent e-mails to all three for more information.

Luckily, Kilimanjaro Adventure Travel (http://www.kilimanjaro.com) replied the same day. We sent a few e-mails back and forth, and requested a list of previous clients. Sitting at the computer, we contacted all of them. The majority had only good things to say about the company and their experiences in Africa (see Appendix II).

We booked a Kilimanjaro climb and a safari right from the computer screen. We were amazed at how easy it was. Of course, we still had to make flight arrangements, which we did the old-fashioned way, through our travel agent.

With the logistics taken care of, we needed visas for Kenya and Tanzania and vaccinations. Visas were easy—we simply sent our passports along with a multi-page application and the appropriate fee to the respective embassies and they stamped them with a current visa.

We later learned why the visa consisted of a stamp. The application asks for an inordinate amount of information, including the obvious: name, address, date of birth, nationality, plus purpose of visit, length of stay, etc.

Then it really becomes obvious that bureaucrats generate these applications. They ask for means of support while in Africa and if you have enough funds for your stay in Tanzania. As if someone from the United States might have the lunatic idea of emigrating to East Africa to take advantage of their "luxurious" social welfare state. Per capita income in those countries is about three to four hundred dollars per year, compared to over $25,000 in the U.S.

Vaccinations were a little more involved. Diane contacted our local Public Health Department and was informed that they did not offer the types of vaccinations required for Africa. Through our family physician, she contacted the International Travel Center at our hospital, which was more than competent to handle destinations anywhere in the world.

We went to the clinic for an appointment at the travel office. The travel center coordinator was a nurse with a World Health certification. She sat us down in her office and gave us a little background on the various vaccinations required for Kenya and Tanzania, which took about an hour.

The vaccinations included Hepatitis A, Meningococcal to prevent meningitis, an e/PV booster to prevent polio, and a Typhin Vi to prevent typhoid fever. Diane also needed a tetanus booster.

The nurse stamped our vaccination certificates for cholera, although she indicated the cholera vaccine was ineffective and recommended against it.

As we sat there and listened to this list of exotic diseases, I kept wondering what we were getting ourselves into. Meningitis, polio, typhoid fever — these were all diseases from jungle stories and a previous time. Then it hit me that we were really going into the depths of the Dark Continent.

On top of the vaccinations, we had to take a weekly dose of Lariam for the prevention of malaria, starting three weeks before the trip to assess our bodies' reactions to the medicine. The side effects of this medication were listed as upset stomach, stomach pain, nausea, vomiting, diarrhea, headache, insomnia, or lightheadedness. Also there might be unexplained anxiety, mood changes, depression, restlessness, or confusion. Well, I started to develop slight anxiety and I had not even started taking the medication.

We all rolled up our sleeves and received the shots. Diane got five, I got four, and Kyle got three. Diane got the full complement of shots. I already had a current tetanus booster, a consequence of the terrible fall on Popo, and Kyle had current polio and tetanus boosters, so we were spared a few shots.

As it turned out, none of us had side effects from the Lariam. However, Lariam and altitude do not mix. So we didn't take it on the mountain, but postponed the scheduled dose until we had descended.

The medical doctor came in for a little pep talk. He said, "Remember it's not important to make the top. If symptoms of high-altitude sickness appear, it's best to turn around and head back down." Well, he obviously didn't understand climbers very well. Why else would they continue climbing when they were vomiting and having severe migraine headaches if reaching the top was not important. In extreme cases High Altitude Pulmonary Edema or High Altitude Cerebral Edema develops and death occurs. Even this possibility is not enough to stop most climbers.

Of course, it was good medical advice. Kyle was the first to speak up, "What do you mean, Doc, making the top is everything." I quickly added, "We appreciate the good advice, but you're talking to the wrong group. We're headed for the top of Kilimanjaro and we won't let a little altitude bother us." He smiled and left the room. For the next couple of days we had sore arms, but no other side effects from the shots or medication.

Outdoor adventure and mountaineering activities are no longer a cult phenomenon performed by a few deranged daredevils or adrenaline fiends. Ostensibly normal people, including high school teachers, accountants, scientists, and folks from all walks of life participate in mountaineering adventures, even though there is still a serious element of risk in these endeavors.

Ernest Hemingway said that there are only three real sports: automobile racing, bull fighting, and mountain climbing. These three seemingly unrelated sporting activities involve either highly engineered, high-tech machinery; a large aggressive animal with a pair of deadly horns; or a single determined individual with some specialized equipment.

On close inspection, there is a common thread to these seemingly disparate athletic activities — the element of risk. In most other sports, a mistake results in a dropped ball or the loss of a point. In these three sports, a small mistake can have disastrous consequences, including injury or death.

This does not mean that enthusiasts of these sports are suicidal thrill seekers. Rather the element of risk adds to the attraction for participants and observers. We like spectator sports as much as the next person, but we are more inclined to be participants than bystanders.

The turning point for taking the sport of mountain climbing from the few serious, extremely dedicated mountaineers and presenting it to less knowledgeable "weekend" climbers occurred in 1985. That is when fifty-five year old Dick Bass became the first person to climb the highest peak on each of the seven continents, commonly referred to as the "Seven Summits."

Bass, a wealthy entrepreneur from Texas, had virtually no climbing experience. He and Frank Wells, the late president of the Walt Disney Company, organized expeditions to the various mountains, before it was popular, and overcame great logistical and physical hurdles to achieve their goal.

The accomplishment of summiting the peaks received enormous media attention and was popularized in their book, with Rick Ridgeway, titled appropriately "Seven Summits." This started a whole new industry of novice and elite climbers, who wanted to follow in Bass's footsteps and reach as many of the seven summits as their limited expertise or funds would allow.

There was one other matter to consider, namely getting in shape for the physical strain of the climb. Diane and I made it a point to get into the local mountains every weekend. About two weeks before the Africa trip, I had to present a paper about a solar-powered rocket stage at a scientific conference in Oahu, Hawaii.

Diane and I hopped over to the big island of Hawaii with the intent of climbing Mauna Kea, the highest mountain in the Pacific basin. It's a 4206-meter, extinct volcano with several massive telescopes at the top.

Once in the rental car, we looked at the map the rental car agency gave us, and noticed some instructions on the map, which were also repeated in the rental agreement. It said in big letters: "DO NOT DRIVE ON SADDLE ROAD. YOUR AGREEMENT DOES NOT COVER THE VEHICLE ON THAT ROAD." They must have been kidding, because that was the road to the mountain.

Of course, we ignored the warning and drove straight to Saddle Road to check out the trailhead. We couldn't figure out what their problem was, because it's a perfectly good, well-paved road. It's narrow and curvy, but that just makes the driving more fun. After we located the trailhead, we returned and checked into our bed and breakfast near Volcano Park.

The next day we got to the mountain just before sunrise for our hike. We were the only hikers on Mauna Kea that day, probably because it was perfect beach weather below. Also, a series of paved service roads and a beehive of construction and scientific activity, related to the Keck Telescope Facility, dominate the top and distract from the enjoyment of the mountain. But for us it was good training and altitude acclimatization.

Our jobs had us glued to a desk chair most of the time, so we couldn't train exclusively in the mountains. In addition to hiking and climbing, it was critical to conduct an exercise program that was compatible with our lives and prepared our bodies for the grueling climb.

We followed a serious program that I developed in conjunction with experts in the fitness and climbing communities, which included elements from bodybuilding, resistance training, and cardiovascular exercises to produce measurable results. This program used both free weights and exercise machines, and plenty of aerobic exercises, including circuit training, stair master, treadmill, jogging, and hiking.

Even though hiking and non-technical climbing stresses mostly the legs, it is important to develop all the major muscle groups in your body. For example, to carry a heavy backpack you need strong shoulders, in addition to a strong back and abdominal muscles.

The stronger your muscles and the more tuned and responsive your body is, the easier it is to perform difficult climbs and, perhaps more important, the less likely you are to injure yourself or misstep on a critical pitch, which can have disastrous consequences. We used a progressive resistance-training program emphasizing the major muscle groups: legs, calves, chest, back, abdomen, shoulders, and arms.

The exercise routine consisted of a five-day program, in which I worked every body part three times in two weeks, leaving two to three days for the muscle groups to rest and recuperate before blasting them again. Five days of weight training and one day of hiking or climbing left one day of rest to round out the week. The routine consisted of the following schedule, with most sets consisting of 8 to 10 repetitions:

Day One - legs and calves. 4 sets of "Leg Blaster." The Leg Blaster is a specialized piece of equipment designed to work the quadriceps, one of the most important muscle groups for mountain climbing (More information on the Leg Blaster is available through Zane Experience, P. O. Box 4088, La Mesa, CA 91944, or ZANE0001@aol.com).

Three sets for the stubborn calves (straight legs - emphasizing the gastrocnemius, doing 15 to 20 repetitions), 3 sets of leg extensions, 3 sets of leg curls, followed by 15 to 20 minutes on the stair master or treadmill set at an inclined angle to mimic the uphill

Kilimanjaro Adventure 37

effort. These exercises would result in strong legs and tough knees for the mountains.

Day Two - arms, back, calves. 3 sets of calves (bent legs - emphasizing the soleus more than the gastrocnemius, using 15 to 20 repetitions). Working the calves has the additional benefit of strengthening the ankles, which are frequently injured on rough terrain. 3 sets for biceps, 3 sets for triceps, 4 sets for back (e.g., lat machine pulldowns followed by hyperextensions for the spinal erectors in the lower back).

Day Three - chest and shoulders. 2 sets bench press, 2 sets dumbbell or Pec Deck flyes. 4 sets dumbbell shrugs to isolate the trapezius muscles. These muscles are stressed by the shoulder straps of the backpack. 6 sets for shoulders (side laterals - 3 standing and 3 in a prone position). I do not do any type of shoulder presses, because they tend to hurt my shoulder joints.

Every workout was preceded by five to ten minutes of stretching and warm-up. We would finish almost every workout session with 2 to 3 sets of sit-ups and crunches, with about 50 to 100 repetitions, for the abdominals.

Normally one uses a full range of motion when performing weight training to stress the muscle over the entire movement. But the trail in the mountains is never regular and even. To get the muscles used to irregular motions, I used a technique of variable motion sets, particularly for the leg muscles.

For example on the Leg Blaster, I would do four sets, where the first set used only the lower range of motion, the second set used only the upper range of motion and the last two sets used the entire range of motion.

Another way to introduce variety was to alternate between full-range reps and partial-range reps within a set. This way the muscles didn't just get used to the regular motion of the equipment, but had to adapt to some irregularity. In addition to the fitness center workouts, I went for five to ten kilometer runs twice a week, mostly in hilly terrain, where I would have to run uphill and really get used to sucking air, even if it was at sea level.

Diane was concerned about the shape she was in. She worked out regularly in the fitness center, but not as rigorously as she would have liked, and was somewhat derelict in her workout regimen early in the year. She made it to the gym about twice a week and most of her hard training consisted of our weekend hikes. While on Mount Baldy, we talked with some other hikers on the summit and told them of our training for Kilimanjaro.

There was a group of young men in their twenties and one of them told us, "I climbed Kilimanjaro last year and had a good time. Unfortunately, I didn't make the summit. Just about everyone in my group had problems with altitude. We had bad headaches and couldn't keep any food down. We were getting weak and dehydrated, so we had to turn back."

He insisted that altitude problems are more or less statistical and that a certain percentage of people will develop them regardless of conditioning or acclimatization. From what I've read about altitude sickness, it sounded more like he was trying to defend his rationale for not making the summit than espousing real medical science.

The following weekend we went to Baldy again, but the mountain displayed a less hospitable mood. It was engulfed in drizzle and fog, blindingly thick at times. We clambered upward, cautiously groping through the white mist in front of us, until we finally reached the summit. There we encountered the only other person on the soppy mountain. He was a British fellow named Thierry who was training for a climb on Mount McKinley. He had climbed Kilimanjaro three years ago.

He said, "It was the best experience I've ever had. It took me over seven hours from the last hut to the summit and it was freezing cold. I didn't have gloves, so instead I put two pairs of socks over my hands. But it didn't work! My hands and fingers were brutally cold and have been sensitive to the cold ever since then. Of the fourteen people in my group, only three made the top. I hadn't trained very much and really struggled to make the summit." He looked at least ten years younger than we did, but in similar shape. We were also getting some last minute pointers on gear, clothes, sleeping bags, etc.

As we continued to train, Diane almost had her worst fear come true—that she would injure herself while training and not be able to do Kilimanjaro. One evening, we went out for a night on the town. She was dressed up and wearing one of her highest and sexiest pair of heels. Unfortunately, later in the evening she twisted her foot and felt her ankle give way with a sudden snap.

When it happened, she immediately knew she had hurt her ankle and thought, "Oh no, I probably sprained my ankle and won't be able to walk or train for weeks." The next day we had a long hike planned, permits and all, with a couple of hiking buddies.

As bad luck would have it, Diane could barely walk in the morning, let alone get her hiking boots on. When our friends showed up at our house at the crack of dawn, they took one look at her ankle and went back home to resume their abbreviated slumber.

Diane rested that day, iced the ankle, and was able to go for a hike the following day. She could feel her sore ankle during the hike, especially while descending. We had chosen a particular trail on Baldy because of its steep scree field. She compensated for her injury, which then made other parts of her hiked-out legs sore. Not only was her injured ankle sore, now her overstressed knees were hurting. She was really worried about how all this was going to affect her ability to train and perform on Kilimanjaro, but she pretty much kept it to herself.

For the climb on Mauna Kea, she was not a hundred percent yet. As luck would have it, Mauna Kea is not particularly steep or difficult and her tender knees were not heavily taxed. Diane's knee problem would not go away. It would get worse.

Kyle's training program was less structured, but nonetheless fairly involved. He goes surfing regularly, is physically active, and in good shape. For two months before the trip, he went to the fitness center a couple of times per week and worked mainly on his legs, mimicking the routine described above. Being a teenager, it was difficult for him to find the time or the interest to go to the mountains with his parents, just for training.

He told us, "Either I'm strong enough, or I'm not. All the previous times I've been in the mountains I've performed well, including on Whitney. Dad, remember when we went to Whitney with Roko? You and I summited, but he had difficulties. He went so slowly that he barely reached Discovery Pinnacle and didn't even get close to the summit. He climbed Kilimanjaro a few years ago and I figure if he can make it, I can too. I bet I can summit Kilimanjaro."

I just looked at him quizzically, because there was no sense in trying to argue with that kind of teenage logic. For several weeks before the trip, he did accompany us on a few hikes in the mountains for altitude training.

3

The Mountain

Before embarking on an expedition as complex as climbing Kilimanjaro, we needed to do a little homework. So we went to the library, checked out a few books on the subject, and started studying.

Our knowledge of the various trails and climbing conditions was scant; we were even more ignorant of the procedures and necessary permits. It turns out that there are five official routes leading to the top of Kibo, the main peak of Kilimanjaro. We had to decide which one to take.

It had to be a route that was both interesting and challenging. But it couldn't be too tough, because although Kyle is young and strong, he had not trained much. Also, Diane's ankle was still bothering her and we were worried that after a few days on the mountain the pain might flare up again.

The trails are mostly on the south side of the mountain. Starting in a clockwise fashion from the southeast, they are the

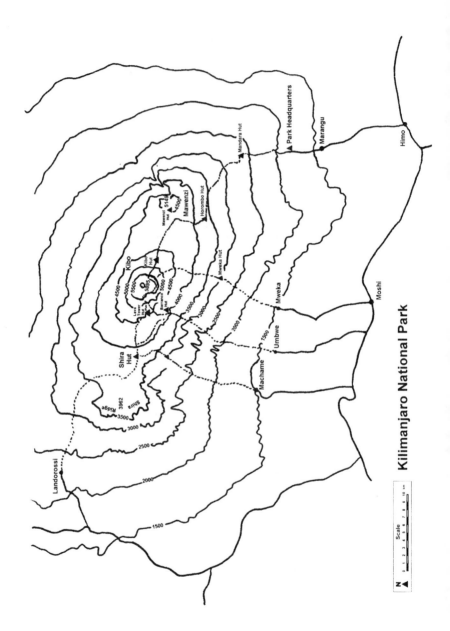

Kilimanjaro Adventure

Marangu route, the Mweka route, the Umbwe route, the Machame route, and almost on the west side of the mountain is the Shira route. Guides are mandatory on all the routes.

The main route up the mountain is called the Marangu trail and is sometimes referred to as the tourist route because it is so heavily trafficked. This route is clearly marked all the way to the top. It is normally a five-day round trip, although many people choose to add an extra day for acclimatization at the Horombo huts at 3720 meters.

The route starts at the park headquarters at the Marangu Gate (1800 meters) where permits are obtained. The first day is a short hike along a narrow trail through thick forest to the Mandara huts at 2700 meters.

The second day takes you through a short section of forest, passes by the Maundi Crater, and then abruptly leaves the forest behind. The trail enters the moorland where you traverse over numerous ridges and ravines until you reach the Horombo huts at 3720 meters.

The third day the trail forks into an upper and lower route. The upper route is shorter, but because it's stony and eroded the guides do not use it much. The lower route takes you through the saddle and merges with the other route near the Kibo hut at 4703 meters.

From there you ascend a steep scree field to the crater rim near Gillman's Point and continue to the summit. It was interesting to note that the first successful climb of Kilimanjaro by Hans Meyer occurred via this route, but we were looking for something with a little more flair.

The Mweka route is the shortest route to the summit and is therefore the steepest and fastest. The trailhead is at the College of Wildlife Management at 1400 meters. The first part of the route is through the forest along an old logging track, then through a natural gully to the Mweka huts at 3000 meters.

The trail meanders through the southeast valley to the Barafu huts at 4600 meters. From Barafu, the ascent takes you through a gap in the southern ice fields to the crater rim, just west of Stella Point. Then, follow the crater rim to Uhuru Peak.

Another steep, short route is the Umbwe trail. The trailhead is at the Umbwe Mission, northwest of Moshi. The initial part of the climb takes you through the forest and then along a narrow ridge between the Lonzo and Umbwe rivers. The first primitive campsite is at Bivouac I at 2800 meters, the next at Bivouac II at 3780 meters.

The trail continues along a ridge to the Barranco hut at 3900 meters, which is not used much, because better shelter is found a half-hour up the trail in the form of some spacious caves in the Barranco Wall. The trail joins the Machame trail before the Western Breach, and then it is a short hike to Uhuru Peak.

The Machame route is considered to be the most scenic route up Kilimanjaro. You reach the trailhead by driving west of Moshi and turning north through the village of Machame and some coffee plantations. The trail meanders through dense forest to the Machame huts at 3000 meters.

It then continues along a steep ridge and through a gorge to the Shira hut. The climb takes you past the Lava Towers and up the Western Breach to Uhuru Peak. The descent is normally taken along the Marangu route. Most overnight stays are in tents carried by porters. Six days are required for this route.

A completely different approach is along the Shira route, through the Shira Plateau on the west side of the mountain. The trailhead is only accessible by four-wheel drive on a dirt road outside of the village of Londorossi. The trail begins in a forest planta-

Kilimanjaro Adventure

tion, followed by natural forest, before it opens up to the moorland. The Shira hut is located at 3840 meters. From there, the trail leads to the Lava Tower where it joins the Machame route.

We decided to take the Machame route, because from everything we had read and heard it is the most scenic and it is less traveled than the Marangu route. Of course, now we had to take care of all the logistics.

Kyle was attending summer school that year. Between the end of summer school and the beginning of the new school year, Kyle's senior year, there was plenty of time for the trip. After Diane and I checked our work schedules, we tried to squeeze in some time off for this expedition.

These days Diane manages a group of writers for a company that designs and manufactures equipment for the semiconductor industry. This demanding office job is a stark contrast to mountain climbing and requires substantial planning to integrate with our backcountry escapades.

We also checked the phases of the moon. We wanted to have a full or near full moon for the summit attempt, which occurred on August 18. Then we had to work airline travel around that time period. Airline travel proved to be a limiting factor, as was time off from our jobs.

Because of the late date for booking airfare, we were limited to our arrival and departure dates. Taking the days required for transfers between airports, hotels, and the safari we planned to build into the trip, we had only five days to complete the climb of the mountain.

If we considered only "standard" climbing packages arranged by the park authorities, we were limited to the Marangu route or one of the minor routes. We discussed it and decided that although the Marangu was not the most challenging or scenic route, it would work best for us and our schedules. We would have our teenage son with us and keeping a teenager entertained can be challenging.

We hoped, that by some luck of the draw, there might be another teenager on the mountain and that was more likely on the Marangu trail. So much for flair. When planning with a group, compromises have to be made. Therefore, August 20 would be our summit day, and we would have a nearly full moon. We settled on the Marangu Route, a decision that with any luck would not come back to haunt us.

With the choice of routes settled, I continued reading about the mountain, absorbing information vital to a successful climb. I discovered which months were the rainy seasons and what to expect in terms of temperature as you ascend the mountain.

There were a few other items of interest that popped up, such as what the name Kilimanjaro means, and how and when the height was measured. We were going to spend several days on the mountain, subjecting ourselves to all kinds of hardships, so we were glad to learn a little bit about it first.

Unlike most other tall mountains, Kilimanjaro is not in a mountain range, but majestically rises almost 5000 meters out of the African savanna. It is only 330 kilometers south of the equator, but has a permanent snow cover and gleaming glaciers crowning its peak. Located in Tanzania, it is the highest mountain on the African continent. It consists of three extinct volcanoes: Shira at 3962 meters, Mawenzi at 5149 meters, and Kibo at 5895 meters.

The top of Kibo is a large, relatively flat expanse of land with three permanent ice fields on the eastern, southern, and northern edges. The summit is called Uhuru Peak. A huge central crater, the Reusch Crater, is the last remnant of a volcanic eruption. Within this crater is the deep Ash Pit, which is composed of volcanic shale and gravel and is generally free of snow and ice due to heat generated by volcanic activity.

The name Kilimanjaro has no clear origin or meaning in Swahili or any other African language. One line of reasoning is that the name originated from a combination of Kiswahili, the language of the Bantu people of Zanzibar off the Indian Ocean coast, and the language of the Arab traders who settled on the East African coast.

The two root words could be "kilima" and "ngaro". Kilima is derived from the word "mlima", which means mountain. However, the addition of the "ki" invokes the diminutive, so "kilima" means small mountain or hill. Perhaps this is out of respect for something so large, similar to giving the nickname "Tiny" to a big guy.

The origin of the "njara" root word is even less obvious and could have several meanings. For the Bantu, "njaro" is the name for a demon that causes extreme cold. On the other hand, the Masai people in the plains use the word "ngare" for water or source of water. And in Swahili, "jaro" means caravan. The theory is that the mountain served as a landmark for caravans traveling to the interior from the coast.

Another interpretation comes from the Kichagga language of the Chagga people, who inhabit the fertile slopes of Kilimanjaro. The word "kilema" means: "He who strikes a blow or strikes one down." The Chagga attempted to climb the mountain early on and many froze to death or were forced to turn back due to the cold and altitude. And the word "njara" means caravan, implying the mountain could strike down caravans of people.

Perhaps the Chagga were trying to tell people interested in the mountain that it was impossible to climb. The Chagga definitely had names for the two most prominent peaks. They called the higher, snow-capped peak "Kibo," which means spotted. It seems very appropriate due to the striations of the white ice against the dark rock. The lower peak was called Kimawense, which means jagged or serrated and is very appropriate for this highly sculpted rock. This turned into Mawenzi among the caravans and other tribes.

The name of the peak, Uhuru, means freedom in Swahili. Tanzania was proclaimed an independent nation in 1964, when the two nations of Tanganyika and Zanzibar united. Tanganyika had already achieved independence in 1961 and in honor of that event, the Tanzanian flag and a symbolic torch of freedom were placed on the summit and the summit was christened Uhuru Peak.

There are two agencies in the United States that keep track of the altitude of mountains, the United States Geological Survey and the National Imaging and Mapping Agency. Between them, they measure the altitudes of mountains, at least in the US, and keep track of accepted altitudes for international mountains.

Accurate measurements of terrain are important to mountaineers, but are mostly made for practical applications such as airline safety and defense purposes. Pilots abhor the idea that a mountain might rise up to meet their airplane unexpectedly.

There is an internationally accepted height of mountains, but there is no standardized method for measuring them. The USGS publishes terrain information on standard map series on a variety of scales. The government in power for a given country reports the names and elevations of mountains to the USGS.

Nowadays elevations are determined by satellite imaging using the Global Positioning System, or simply GPS. Before GPS there were a number of ways to measure altitudes, but mostly it was performed by very careful trigonometric surveys.

Hans Meyer first measured the height of Kilimanjaro in 1889. He took barometric pressure readings with an aneroid and calculated the height to be 6010 meters. It was therefore considered to be an official 6000-meter mountain, even with later measurements to the contrary.

For example, in 1907 the German-English border commission performed a trigonometric survey and determined the height to be 5889 meters. In 1921, C. Gillman measured the height from boiling point readings to be 5965 meters. The privileged 6000-meter status was officially lost on September 18, 1952, when a government-sponsored survey by the Dar Es Salaam Survey Division measured the height to be 5895 meters, which became the internationally accepted height.

Because of its location on the equator, the local topography, and prevailing winds, the climate around Kilimanjaro results in a dry savanna landscape. The mountain is so large that the climate changes drastically with altitude. The lower slopes of the mountain receive considerable rainfall and percolation from the higher regions. These areas are heavily cultivated with grassland and cropland, including coffee and banana plantations.

There are two rainy seasons on Kilimanjaro. The main one is from April to June and a secondary one from October to November. Although the mountain can be climbed year round, there are two main climbing seasons: one is from December to March.

This climbing period is usually dry and may have brief rain showers in the lower, forested regions. The other climbing period is from June through August, which is the main dry season. During this period, it can be very cold at night even at the lower altitudes.

The days are generally clear, but in August and September, clouds can be expected. The summit has typical Arctic conditions, with subfreezing temperatures, very cold winds, and clear skies. The lower-lying valleys and savanna are frequently shrouded in clouds with neighboring mountain peaks rising above the billowing clouds.

The giant crater of Kibo has numerous noteworthy features. It is a large, relatively flat plateau with three distinct glacial ice fields. Since Hans Meyer's first successful summit ascent, the glaciers have been retreating steadily and more regions of the crater are free of ice.

It was not until 1927 that the missionary Dr. Richard Reusch explored the crater region of Kibo and discovered the inner crater, now called the Reusch Crater. The year before he had also discovered the frozen body of a leopard near the top, which was made famous by Ernest Hemingway in his short story "The Snows of Kilimanjaro." All this trivia wasn't terribly exciting, but I suspected that some of it would come in handy once we were on the mountain.

4

Approaching the Mountain

The marathon flight started in San Diego and took us to JFK Airport in New York. The second leg was a non-stop flight from New York to Johannesburg, South Africa, which took the better part of a day — fourteen hours.

We struggled to keep ourselves sane and entertained with magazines, in-flight movies, and books. But then the opportunity presented itself for Diane and me to join the mile-high club. It was pure impulse, but circumstances were too inviting to pass up the chance for some exciting privacy.

The lavatories in most planes are barely large enough to perform the business they were designed for, but our Boeing 747-400 had one that was particularly spacious and allowed for extra-curricular activity. It just proves that even after eighteen years of marriage there is still some room for experimentation if your mind is inventive enough.

We just hoped that having too much fun on the plane on our

way to the mountain didn't somehow anger the spirits of the mountain. After all, according to the native language Kilimanjaro means: "He who strikes one down." We're not superstitious, but there was no reason to force the issue.

We also had plenty of time to read; I had brought some books about Kilimanjaro and enjoyed reading some of the history of the mountain. It turned out to be quite interesting and once we got to the mountain, it had a nice personal touch associated to it.

The exploration of the mountain is knitted into the annals of Africa. The time frame was between 1850 and 1900, when Britain developed an intense interest in the exploration of East Africa. Economic incentives included locating new sources of raw materials and develop new markets for the exchange of goods.

Inland exploration was driven mainly by missionary and scientific ambitions of Britain and Germany. Two German missionaries, Johann Krapf and Johannes Rebmann, set up the first missionary stations in the inland region of East Africa to spread the Gospel and investigate reports of a great white mountain by the caravan leader Bwana Kheri.

Johannes Rebmann and his caravan approached the mountains of the Chaggaland and then became the first European to see Kilimanjaro. He published his account in the *Church Missionary Intelligencer* in April 1849 as follows:

> " ...at about ten o'clock I thought I saw one of them enveloped in a prominent white cloud. My guide simply described the whiteness that I saw, as cold; and it was as good as certain to me that it could be nothing other than snow. They did not want to believe me,

Kilimanjaro Adventure

with the exception of my guide, who, during his last visit to the Chagga, had for a small reward sent some of them up the mountain to bring as much of its silver back to him as they could.

However, they had brought nothing more than water back to the eagerly waiting Swahili. All the strange stories of a gold and silver mountain in the interior, inaccessible on account of evil spirits, which Dr. Krapf and myself had often heard since my arrival on the coast, now suddenly became clear to me.

Naturally, the fact that the unaccustomed cold had rapidly forced the half-naked visitors to the mountain to return, or had indeed actually killed them, was attributed by the natives in their ignorant state to the power of evil spirits."

Rebmann's report was received with astonishing interest and a healthy dose of skepticism. The greatest criticism came from the English geographer William Cooley, which was published in the *Atheneum* journal.

In that report, Cooley questioned the observational powers of Rebmann and Krapf and their intellectual capabilities to conclude something as absurd as a snow-capped mountain at the equator.

The first serious attempt to climb the mountain came in 1861 by the German explorer Baron Karl von der Decken. Two attempts along the west side of the mountain failed to get higher than 2600 meters.

Von der Decken returned the following year with Otto Kersten for another attempt, this time from the south through Moshi. The ruler of Moshi was Mandara, and after some negotiating, he provided guides for the two explorers. Von der Decken and Kersten continued despite severe headaches and weakness to an altitude of almost 4000 meters, before they were forced to turn back due to hypothermia.

The English missionary, Charles New, met Baron von der Decken in 1871 on his travels to Moshi and decided to investigate Kilimanjaro in some detail. After one failed attempt, he and a guide reached the snow line on the southeast side of Kibo. At that time the glacier fields were larger than they are now and it is estimated that he ascended to just over 4000 meters. He returned in 1873 for further study when he encountered resistance by Mandara, who took everything the missionary had. This forced New to turn back and he became ill and died before he reached Mombasa.

In 1884, the British Association for the Advancement of Science and the Royal Geographical Society jointly financed a six-month study of the mountain by the Scottish naturalist Sir Harry Johnston. Among other studies, he was to investigate the colonial prospects of the fertile Kilimanjaro district, where he started a concession at Taveta and the cultivation of wheat and coffee.

Johnston made his first attempt up the mountain from Moshi. With Mandara's assistance, he was able to ascend to 2800 meters before encountering a hostile attack by a neighboring tribe.

His second major attempt was through the village of Marangu, where he set up several camps, the last at about 3000 meters. From there, he pushed for the summit with three porters. The porters stayed behind in a cave on a hill at the edge of the saddle. He proceeded up the steep cone of Kibo, but before reaching the crater rim had to return to the cave, which had already been abandoned by the porters.

At about this time back in Europe, Germany's Chancellor Bismarck reversed his position on colonial policy and adopted an

Kilimanjaro Adventure

expansionist strategy for Germany. Within a year, Bismarck annexed Cameroon, Togo, South West Africa, and northern New Guinea. Johnston's findings, regarding the economic value of the Kilimanjaro district, created fear of German annexation of East Africa.

Indeed, Germany established a Protectorate that included Chagga and Kilimanjaro. In negotiations over territories between Germany, England, France, and the Sultan of Zanzibar, borders were established. Kaiser Wilhelm wanted Kilimanjaro to be on German territory, because Johannes Rebmann, a German, discovered it.

Supposedly Queen Victoria gave Kilimanjaro to her grandson as a birthday present in 1886 and therefore had to realign the border. These negotiations and the royal "gift" explain the kink in the border just east of Kilimanjaro.

Dr. Hans Meyer, a geology professor at the University of Leipzig, visited Kilimanjaro and made his first summit attempt in August 1887. He took Johnston's route from Marangu to the saddle before scaling the east side of the cone of Kibo.

Meyer continued despite being trapped in a snowstorm to an altitude of 5500 meters, where he encountered a punishing wall of solid glacier ice and was forced to abandon his goal of reaching the summit. Meyer's second expedition was even less successful, and he did not even reach the mountain before having to turn around due to problems with the native tribes.

Hans Meyer's third serious expedition to Kilimanjaro occurred in 1889; this time he was accompanied by one of the most experienced alpine mountaineers of the time, Ludwig Purtscheller. In Marangu, they chose a crew of six natives: a guide, an assistant guide, and four porters to help with the monumental efforts of the climb. This unrelenting group established a base camp at the foot of the mountain and then a midway camp on the Maue stream at 2900 meters, at the upper edge of the forest.

They set up regular shuttles of supplies to the upper camp, which allowed them to stay and acclimatize at the higher altitude. Their equipment included warm woolen clothes, snow glasses and masks, crampons, ice axes, ropes, tents, and sleeping bags made of sheepskin.

From the midway camp, Meyer and Purtscheller took two days to reach the saddle. They ascended via the southeast side of the Kibo cone, reached the ice field, and climbed the glacier wall. After three hours of extremely exhausting work, they traversed the jagged ice and reached the crater rim.

They realized immediately that they had not attained the summit, as they could observe that to the south. Without the proper gear and due to the late hour, they had to return to the Kibo camp. For a second attempt at the summit, they recognized that they needed a higher camp. They found it in the form of a cave at 5150 meters, which is now called the Hans Meyer cave.

The following day they assaulted the summit with renewed vigor. They ascended the glacier as before to the crater rim and then climbed along the outer crater wall to the summit of Kibo. At 10:30 A.M. on October 6, 1889, Hans Meyer became the first person to stand atop Kibo.

For the next twenty years, no expeditions reached the summit, although numerous attempts were made. In 1898, Captain Kurt Johannes, the military commander of the German colonial army in Moshi, succeeded in reaching the crater rim.

Since Hans Meyer had reached the summit eleven years prior, some of the glacial ice had retreated and exposed a distinctive narrow pass in the crater rim. The newly discovered landmark was named the Johannes Notch and is where the climbers who use the Marangu trail first reach the crater rim. Several more expeditions, both for scientific and increasingly for sporting reasons, reached the summit, until the First World War curtailed any interest in the mountain. After the war, it took until 1921 for the first serious expedition to scale Kilimanjaro, this time led by the English geographers C. Gillman and P. Nason. Both of them reached the crater rim, but were too exhausted to continue. They planted their Union Jack, intended for the summit, in a flat, rocky outcrop near the Johannes Notch. That landmark became known as Gillman's Point. It is a popular destination for many of today's climbers.

If reading all that in gory detail seemed interesting, you can imagine how long the flight was. But finally, after all the reading, movies, and airplane food, we were overjoyed to be on firm ground in Johannesburg. The airport was clean and located in a busy commercial district.

We could see our hotel from the airport. The whole setting could have been in a medium-sized town in the USA. Since this was our first visit to Africa, we didn't know what to expect, but so far so good.

The only problem was that my nose was stuffed up. Was it from the air in the airplane? I asked both Diane and Kyle about how they felt and they said they noticed a little stuffiness in the plane, but it seemed to have cleared up on the ground. I was a little worried, because on the last day at work, my boss called me into his office for a closed-door meeting to give him a briefing on the status of all my programs.

A colleague and I had just invented a corrosion-resistant surface treatment for Pitot tubes. Pitot tubes are devices that are mounted on the nose of airplanes. They are used to measure air pressure that is converted to an electrical signal, which tells the pilot how fast the plane is going.

In addition to optimizing the technology, we were working on two patents in the U.S. and one in France for various aspects of our invention. I had arranged for these activities to continue on autopilot.

Another project I managed was to develop a composite target chamber for a fusion power reactor. Nuclear fusion is the process that powers the sun and stars, and is being studied for terrestrial power plants of the future. This is a major program sponsored by the Department of Energy and required careful delegation to ensure progress in my absence.

The problem was that my boss was blowing his nose profusely and spreading his germs. He was complaining that his young daughter had spread her cold to him. Great, so he had to show up and spread his to everyone else, including me. Although I tried to keep my distance across the table, could I have possibly picked up a bug? A cold with a stuffed up nose was the last thing I needed on the mountain.

Dinner conversation at the hotel restaurant centered on mountain climbing and Kilimanjaro. Kyle wondered, "Why is Gillman's Peak called a peak if Uhuru is the real peak?" "Actually it's called Gillman's Point," I reminded him, "and it's just a landmark on the crater rim." We joked that it should have been called Gillman's Intermediate Peak, or Gillman's Turnaround Point, or Gillman's Quitting Point.

Of course, it was easy to say those things sitting in a fancy restaurant in Johannesburg. Then he declared, "I definitely want to make Uhuru Peak, since that's the real summit." I just hoped he really meant it, because I know it is mental toughness more than anything else that gets you up mountains. My son, like most teenagers, rarely conveyed a sense of determination for anything other than skateboarding or hanging out at the mall or the movies. Scientists like me get excited over the strangest things. Just for fun, when we returned to the room we filled the sink with water and pulled the plug. The vortex that formed was in a clockwise fashion, as it should be on the southern hemisphere. This is opposite to the counterclockwise vortex formed on the northern hemisphere.

The vortex forms due to the Coriolis force exerted on the water by the rotation of the earth. This force is in opposite directions for the northern and southern hemispheres resulting in the opposite vortex formation. I first learned this in high school physics and it took twenty-five years to get to the southern hemisphere and personally make the observation.

We barely slept that night in Johannesburg due to the time change and we figured we would make up for it the next night. Little did we realize how long it would take to overcome the eleven-hour time difference and the problems it would create.

For the flight to Nairobi, we asked for a seat assignment on the right side of the plane. On our map, it looked like our approach into Nairobi would give us a view of Kilimanjaro from that side of the plane.

As we flew north toward Kenya and Tanzania, we encountered a thick layer of clouds and we were concerned that we might not get to see the mountain at all. Shortly before Nairobi, the pilot announced that Kilimanjaro would be visible on the left side of the plane in a few more minutes and it should make a good photo opportunity. So much for planning a view out the right side of the plane.

Everyone grabbed their cameras and rushed to the left side of the plane. With all the weight being transferred to that side of the plane, you could almost sense the pilot struggling to keep the plane level.

Sure enough, we noticed some mountainous peaks directly ahead of us. A crater rim was visible through the clouds. It was a lot more jagged than I imagined and less impressive than I thought it would be.

But a good portion of it was engulfed in the cloud cover and perhaps that masked enough of the mountain to conceal its size. I took a couple of pictures and really didn't know what to think of it.

Then a passenger, who frequently flew this route, mentioned, "That's not Kilimanjaro, but Mount Meru. Kilimanjaro will be visible in a couple more minutes." I was glad to hear that we had made a mistake, because I'd hate to think that we had come all this way for that sad looking volcano.

Diane was a little slower getting out of her seat. She was still fumbling with the buckle of her seat belt when she noticed that Kyle and I were already looking out the window. She says that I was out of my seat before the pilot had finished the sentence describing the view we would have of the mountain. And that Kyle flew or levitated over her seat. A friendly woman sitting across from Diane in a window seat, motioned her to come over and get a look.

This woman began casual conversation with Diane, "Your husband and son are quite interested in seeing Kilimanjaro." To which Diane replied, "Yeah, we've trained for months and came all the way from San Diego to climb it." And she said, "Oh I did it, about seven years ago — it was great — hard work, grueling, and all, but I climbed it."

Diane congratulated her, and when she was not looking she quickly sized her up. "Okay. Let me see, she's at least five to

Kilimanjaro Adventure

ten years older than me, and about . . ." Later it occurred to Diane that the woman never did say which trail she took and if she reached Uhuru Peak or Gillman's Point or how far she actually ascended the mountain.

Climbing and summiting are two different things and in casual conversation can be confused.

We had sneaked into the first class cabin and were crowded around the oval window, holding our breath in anticipation. Then the real Kilimanjaro came into sight. We were almost directly over it, so we had to press our faces against the cold window and look almost straight down.

It was so immense that it almost interfered with the flight path of the plane. If it had been any higher, the pilot would have been forced to fly around it instead of over it. There was a sea of clouds that the icy peak and volcanic crater punctured to reveal its might. "Oh my god," Diane gasped. Kyle and I were saying things like, "Look at it!" "Wow, it's awesome."

The snow-covered south face and squared off peak were the first features we noticed. The top of the mountain is a huge plateau that looks relatively flat and is covered almost entirely with snow. The deep central crater was dark and free of snow and was a marked contrast to the surrounding expanse of white. The large Eastern and Northern Icefields were gleaming in a brilliant blue. It looked nothing like other volcanoes we had seen in Mexico or Hawaii.

As the plane moved over the giant mountain, we could see where the crater wall stood above all else. It was staring us in the face, Uhuru Peak — our goal. In addition, there was what looked like a wide trail leading up from a hut. Yes, we could see the Kibo hut and the infamous scree field. Scree is gravel-like, loose volcanic rock. We visually studied the scree field.

Awe-inspiring view of Kilimanjaro, the highest peak in Africa.

It appeared to extend straight up for about half the distance from the hut to the rim with no discernible features. Toward the upper part, we could see numerous switchbacks. That was a good sign. If there were switchbacks that meant the terrain was solid enough to maintain a trail.

Of course, the route traversed the open scree field where there was no visible trail. That part turned out to be problematic later during the climb. The angle was difficult to judge from directly overhead, but it looked very steep.

By now, we got the impression that the belly of the plane was almost scraping along the summit. We were within spitting distance of the crater and the destination of our mountaineering expedition.

All of us continued to gaze at the mountain and Kyle remarked, "It looks so close, what do you think it'll be like to be stand-

Kilimanjaro Adventure

ing on Uhuru Peak?" "It'll be a lot different than you think," I responded. "The real feelings have to be earned with hard work. Sort of like buying an Olympic gold medal at a pawnshop versus competing for one and receiving it on the winners' podium. You won't know until you've actually been there."

All that Kili trivia took on an entirely different perspective. It was not just abstract words in some obscure book anymore, but now we were looking at the real thing and soon we would be struggling with it.

Diane said it looked impressive, but remained relatively quiet. That was not a good sign, and I thought that she must be concerned about the size of the mountain. I was right, because she was thinking, "Kyle and Hal are so excited, as if they can't wait to get on the mountain. They're practically salivating at the sight. The mountain looks so big and ominous and the glacial ice cap gives it the impression we are on an expedition to the Arctic pole."

When we passed the mountain and returned to our seats, Kyle and I were still talking about how we had a great view of the mountain, the trail, the scree field, etc. Sensing Diane's distress I leaned close to her and asked, "Babe, you're so quiet, is something wrong?"

She was thinking, Hell yes, something's wrong. Did you see the size of that mountain? Did you see how steep the scree field was? This is much bigger and steeper than Popocatepetl, remember Popo?

Disguising her concern she said, "Oh I'm okay, it's just that the mountain looks pretty big and I'm a bit overwhelmed by the sight." But her thoughts continued, what an understatement, I should have trained more. I feel unfit for the task. And now I'm worried about my knees and ankle. Maybe it's just a combination of everything. We've been traveling for days, or so it seems. I'm tired, and

Any lower, we'd be landing. Uhuru peak is the highest point on the cliff above the central crater.

now I've seen the mountain, not just pictures, but seen it with my own eyes. I'm just overwhelmed and engulfed in nervous anticipation of the climb.

    A few minutes later we landed in Nairobi. It's a small airport with a wide range of people walking around. People from India, Africa, Asia, and USA— it seemed there were people from every part of the world. We stood in line for passport control and noticed the first mosquitoes buzzing around the passport official.

    So the malaria-spreading mosquitoes were already at the airport to greet us. Or maybe these were trained mosquitoes that gave the passport bureaucrat a hard time, because he gave everyone else a hard time. Perhaps due to the mosquitoes we easily got through passport control and went to the baggage claim area. This consisted of four separate belts that were not well marked, which led to some confusion.

Kyle remarked, "This place is the shabbiest airport I've ever seen. Two of the belts are out of commission and serve as long benches for people to park their butts on." He was right, the place was falling apart.

There were flimsy metal boxes mounted up high on a large I-beam. These boxes had empty spaces in them and remnants of electrical wires for what apparently used to be TV monitors to indicate where your bags should be. It was almost as if these monitors were designed and built with failure in mind and never really were supposed to work.

One belt was moving, but had a sign for another airline. Following our herd instinct we stood there and waited along with familiar people from our flight. After a few minutes, another belt started moving and a crowd of people moved over to wait by that belt. We followed.

This one had a lot of bags from Air India, conveniently identifiable from a band across every suitcase applied by the airline. In between the Air India luggage, were bags from our flight and we recognized our first piece of luggage.

Two more pieces showed up in quick succession. Then we had to wait and wait. I started thinking about what was in the still-missing piece of luggage. Our Thermo-rest pads and hiking boots!

Without that bag, we would be dead in the water. Even if we could buy hiking boots, there would be no time to break them in. New boots can be murder on the feet. Finally, after most people had their bags, the bag containing our boots showed up.

We caught a cab to our hotel in Nairobi. The cab ride was

an adventure in itself. First, they drive on the left side of the road, which for us is the wrong side. And worse, once we got to town we noticed that the traffic was almost completely unregulated by signs and lights.

It was simply a random flow of cars and buses that fought for needed space on the roads. Cars were everywhere; lane lines were completely ignored and cars drove where it was most convenient. Horns honked, cars turned and merged out of nowhere. It was total chaos, but somehow traffic moved and we arrived at the hotel in one piece.

We had a reservation at the Fairview Hotel, in a nice, secluded compound on the edge of downtown Nairobi. We were pleasantly surprised that they actually had our name in the computerized register. The hotel clerk was a well-groomed native who spoke impeccable English with a very British accent. I asked if the surrounding area was safe to walk around in and he responded, "Why, jolly yes."

Our room was in the back with its own private courtyard and entrance. It was very comfortable and the Fairview became our home-away-from-home while we were in Africa. Inside was a small anteroom with a single bed separated by a door to the main room with two single beds and a separate bath.

All the beds had sheer white mosquito nets hanging above them from the ceilings creating protected air space during the night. After we got settled I asked Kyle, "You want to go for a walk with me to check out the neighborhood?" "Do you think it's okay, it looks a little dangerous out there," Kyle replied. "Yes, the desk clerk said it was safe." And away we went.

Walking on the side of the crumbling road was even more tumultous than partaking in traffic in the road. Everybody was looking at us as we wandered by. They looked at our clothes, our shoes, everything. We stood out like sore thumbs, as the only white folks in a sea of African natives. The architectural styles were varied and contradictory. All the large office buildings and apartments were simple and dull, like most buildings built by socialist regimes, but seemed to be of sturdy construction.

Wedged everywhere in between the big buildings and all along the side of the roads were plenty of wooden shacks, about the size and shape of a carport. These shacks seemed to be held together with Band-Aids and bailing wire, and appeared as if the big, bad wolf could knock them down just by giving them a huff and a puff.

To continue our walk we had to cross a busy street. "We'll never get over this road. Obviously pedestrians have no rights here," Kyle insisted. "Patience! Even between these erratic drivers we'll find a gap, " I replied. "I'll be surprised if we make it across with our lives, this traffic's just crazy," he remarked. And then at the next gap we dashed across.

We walked several blocks to Uhuru Park and entered a huge flea market. Vendors had laid down blankets on the ground displaying shabby-looking, mostly secondhand wares for sale. There were hordes of people milling around, doing nothing in particular.

The park was maintained, but not with a lot of care. The grass and plants all needed proper trimming. We encountered lots of people and some of them did not look particularly friendly, but we did not witness any obvious hostility. We strolled around the park for a while before we decided to head back to the hotel.

The majority of people we saw along the way had tattered clothes. The ones coming in and out of nearby office buildings were dressed in nice-looking business attire. A smartly dressed businesswoman got into a big Mercedes and briskly drove away. Next to her parking space was a ditch where a man was kneeling, filling two large plastic jugs with filthy water.

I wondered, "What in the world could that be used for." And Kyle said, "Gross, did you notice that wasn't just a ditch for rain water. It looks more like it's an open sewer line." Obviously even filthy water had some use and value here.

Back at the hotel Diane was worried and thinking, Hal and Kyle were going for a walk, and they asked if I want to go? No way. And it's not a good idea for them either. But my two guys are . . . well, looking for adventure. I told them I'd sit on the terrace and read. Then it occurred to me, the hotel's located in a secluded compound, and is the surrounding area really safe?

All of a sudden, she became concerned about the two of us walking around. A while later, when we showed up at the gated compound, she was relieved. But when we told her about our explorations she wondered about my sanity.

Later that evening, Chris and Avril MacDonald of Rafiki Africa met us to give us a briefing on the events for the next few days. They're a British couple, both forty, who have lived and worked in Nairobi for the last six or seven years.

The name of their company, "Rafiki," means "Friend" in Swahili, and symbolizes their approach to doing business in Africa. It was reassuring for us paranoid Americans, who were in a third-world country for the first time, to be dealing with someone who knew how things work here. We chatted about who we are, what we do, and why we were here.

When Chris learned that Kyle and I had gone for a walk in the immediate neighborhood, he was horrified. He told us, "About a week ago there was unrest here in Nairobi. It was centered in

Kilimanjaro Adventure

Uhuru Park, where you just walked. People were clubbed by the police and one person was killed. He was beheaded and the body was dragged around. In some of the nearby towns, police have been killed by mobs. You've got to be real careful in the cities right now."

We had read a little about it in the newspapers, but chose to brush it off for this visit. But now that we were here, we had to pay attention to it. Chris mentioned that the bad political climate and the unrest had hurt the tourist business that year. Well, it was easy to see why.

Chris filled us in on some of the details of the drive to Kilimanjaro. We had opted for ground transportation to Moshi, rather than flying into the Kilimanjaro International Airport east of Moshi.

We hoped to see a little more of both Kenya and Tanzania that way. A transport company called Davanu would send a bus at 7:30 A.M. and take us to the nearby Norfolk Hotel to meet up with others traveling to Arusha and Moshi. The bus would then drive to the Tanzanian border, which should take about two and a half hours.

After the passport check, we would drive another hour and a half to a large hotel called the Novotel. There we would switch buses and drive to Moshi where we would spend the night at the Springland guesthouse. We would be driven to the mountain the next morning and meet the guide and porters.

It all sounded very organized. He told us about a walking safari that he organizes that sounded wonderful, but it would have to wait for the next time. After they left, we retired for another terrible night's sleep.

Kyle thought that until now Africa was much different from what he had expected. Nairobi was a big city, but not quite like a city in America, for it was full of contrasts. We saw terribly poor people and conditions, and could not even drink the water. Yet some things were similar to back home. There were shops and office buildings and lots of cars in the streets.

Our hotel was nice and comfortable with good service. It had two good restaurants, one inside, and one outside. We had a TV in the room, but only about seven or eight channels, where they showed mostly U.S. shows and movies. The beds were comfortable and the mosquito nets were kind of cool. They really gave the beds and the whole room a foreign or exotic effect.

We got up early so we would be ready for our 7:30 shuttle. We had a quick breakfast and waited for the bus until after 8:00 o'clock. At about 8:30 a Davanu bus showed up. I asked the driver if this was our bus to the Norfolk Hotel and Arusha. He asked, "What's your name?" "Streckert." "No, I'm here for someone else, your name is not on the list." But he was going to the Norfolk and Arusha.

Well, that was close enough for me, so we loaded our gear and hopped on the bus. A man on the bus had overheard my conversation with the driver and he confirmed that this was the right bus.

I said, "They seem to be somewhat disorganized here." And he and his companion, both British, chuckled. With one eyebrow raise, he smirked, "I thought only the British tended toward gross understatements."

At the Norfolk Hotel, a young woman from the Davanu company entered the bus and blurted, "Names, destinations, and tickets." Tickets - nobody told us about tickets and I told her we didn't have tickets. She said, "No tickets, no problem — name please." I asked about the return trip and she said that was no problem either.

Kilimanjaro Adventure

The bus was full, so all the luggage was lifted to the roof of the bus where it was tied down. During the bus rides, we made sure that the luggage was on the same bus as we were. Then we finally left and drove through Nairobi and watched in amazement how the traffic flowed chaotically with a near miss every few moments.

After we left Nairobi and were on the open road, the drive was even more amazing. The bus lurched down the well-maintained road and the driver frequently passed slower cars. Some of those passes occurred on blind turns or with distant on-coming traffic. Because the bus was slow to accelerate, it made for exciting moments to see which driver would yield first.

The ride was fascinating and reassured us that we made the right decision to take the bus. It gave us a great opportunity to see some of the countryside with the people, the buildings, and the animals along the road. We saw Masai tending their herds of cattle in the middle of nowhere.

Near the villages, we frequently saw locals sitting under trees, talking and gesturing. Or women transporting large loads on their backs or gracefully balancing them on their heads.

The architecture in the villages ranged from modern buildings to small shacks made of sticks and mud, but most of them consisted of tin-roofed wooden shacks. Along the road we saw exotic wildlife including zebras, gazelles, camels, antelopes, monkeys, and marabous.

We passed through roadblocks set up by police. We must have passed through at least ten of these between Nairobi and Moshi. They consisted of long heavy boards with spikes sticking straight up set across the lanes so cars would have to weave around them to get through. Every time at least four to six cops were standing around. That was about the only time we saw cops.

These roadblocks were a complete mystery. Kyle asked, "Dad, what do you think those road blocks are for?" "I don't know, they do seem rather useless." Kyle observed, "All the cars and buses simply ignore them and drive around the barriers, if the cops waive them through or not. It makes no sense other than to give the cops the impression that they are working." "Well, maybe that's the answer," I commented, "to give the cops some visibility, and because they don't have a Dunkin Donuts to hang out at."

The drive continued for about three and a half hours until we arrived at the Kenya/Tanzania border town of Namanga. A woman with either the Tanzanian government or the transfer company entered the bus and directed us to the passport office for a visa check and a stamp.

The bureaucrats didn't even look at the pictures in the passports. Then we pushed our way back on the bus and drove about five seconds to the Tanzanian side of the border for another passport check. This time Diane decided to stay on the bus and Kyle and I took her passport with us.

They simply opened the passports, including Diane's, stamped them somewhere near the visas, initialed them and waved us on. Their customs procedures were little more than a charade for the purpose of generating revenues, which really became obvious next.

As I was waiting in line, I noticed a man from India was having some kind of problem with his passport. He and a border official stepped aside, gestured, and argued for a while.

Apparently some stamp was missing or in the wrong place, because they kept flipping the pages in his passport. Then some dollar bills changed hands and the problem went away.

We crossed the border again on the way back and went through the same ritual of getting off the bus and getting exit and

Kilimanjaro Adventure

entry stamps. By the time we left Africa, we counted a total of ten stamps in each of our passports just from this trip. They took their jobs seriously — they wouldn't want to miss placing a stamp somewhere, or collecting a few extra revenues, not to say bribes, on the side.

While waiting on the bus, Diane observed the hoards of locals waiting to descend on the unsuspecting tourists as they exited the refuge of the passport office. The majority of them wore a variety of western-looking clothes, but many wore the local style of clothes.

These are colorful apparel, called Shukas, consisting of a cloth that is wrapped around the torso of both men and women, elegantly draping their bodies. Diane was especially intrigued by the women. Several had a small child wrapped somehow into their Shukas.

Many had shaved their heads and wore large earrings in their ears. The lower parts of the ear lobes were frequently cut and stretched to an unbelievable size. The hole in the ear lobe was so large that a fist could fit through it.

They frequently twisted the extra length of skin over the top of the ear. It was quite eye-catching when worn that way, because it gave the appearance of a miniature Danish stuck over the ears, similar to the way Princess Leia in *Star Wars* rolled up her hair.

Diane tried to capture in her mind how they looked before any of them discovered her staring at them. Because once they see you looking at them, they swarm around you, fervently peddling their goods. The native men and women are quite aggressive about selling their wares to the tourists on the buses.

They can be unrelenting as they do not take "no thanks" easily. And with Diane's curiosity in people watching — well, once they noticed her attention, they flocked to her. The wares are handcrafted jewelry and wood carvings, all very nice, but nothing exceptional. If a person is interested in those types of things, bartering through the window of the bus puts you in a very good position to get things at a good price.

Back to the bus for another three-hour drive to the Novotel Hotel. There nobody seemed to be able to count. They wanted to pack about fifteen people and loads of mountaineering and camping paraphernalia into a small minivan. The confusion was followed by a lot of head scratching.

I struck up a conversation with a German hiker named Berndt, who was on his third or fourth stint to Africa. He filled me in, "Believe it or not, this bus ride is well organized compared to others I've experienced."

Carved masks, rhinos, necklaces, anyone?

Kilimanjaro Adventure

The last trip he had been on, the radiator sprung a leak and they had to stop for water every fifteen minutes. And there aren't a lot of gas stations and well-stocked stores in these areas. That reminded me of the man we had seen in Nairobi filling jugs of water, maybe it was intended for a radiator.

The particular trip Berndt was talking about took an additional twelve hours. Luckily for us a second minivan showed up and the group split up, with the mountain of gear more or less randomly divided among the roofs of the two minivans. We were finally on our way again.

Store front in Namanga. Notice slabs of beef hanging unrefrigerated in window of this butchery.

We noticed a large mountain straight ahead obscured by a thick haze. Was it Kilimanjaro? We looked at it, but couldn't make out enough detail. It looked like Mount Meru again, which meant

Kilimanjaro had to be on our left. There was a solid cloud cover, but on close inspection, we could make out a broad base of a giant mountain. The huge base extended along the dry plains for most of the part of the horizon that we could see.

As the solid cloud cover broke up it exposed a window of blue sky. This was our first chance to see the peak of Kilimanjaro from the ground. It was enormous. The cotton-like clouds interrupted the hulking base, but suspended above the clouds, the snow and ice-covered peak towered with authority high into the brilliant sky.

For most mountains, the difference in elevation between the base and the summit is not so great, because the base is already at considerable altitude.

But for Kilimanjaro, the difference in elevation is almost 5000 meters. This difference is probably the greatest in the world, and if anything, rivaled only by Denali*. So the summit looks extremely high from the ground. For Mount Everest, the difference from the base to the peak is only about 3500 meters.

I gazed at the peak for several minutes, envisioning myself standing on top and looking down. It was difficult to imagine, because the peak extended so high into the sky it looked impossible to scale from where we were. It was more impressive from this perspective than from the plane.

It seemed like an impossible goal, but if all went well we would achieve it in five days. That was a gratifying short-term goal compared to most worthwhile endeavors. For example, it takes a long time to build a house or a bridge; or it can take months to put a business deal together.

* Denali is Mt. McKinley's original Athapaskan name.

Kilimanjaro Adventure

My field is science and it took four years just to earn my doctorate in analytical chemistry at the University of Wisconsin-Madison. Some of my current projects take years to complete. In addition, the degree of success is not always obvious. Some research projects only yield a negative result, or are concluded with a thick final report that nobody reads.

However, in mountaineering, the success or failure of the project is readily measured and typically only takes days or at best weeks to accomplish. The effect is very intense and concentrated, with a strong physical component in addition to the mental and emotional stress. Because of the challenge, coupled with the high degree of uncertainty and risk, the feeling of success is very powerful when the goal is finally reached.

Kyle was staring at the clouds on the horizon, fighting a fatal case of boredom on the long bus ride, when a certain cloud caught his eye. He said, "That cloud looks different from the surrounding ones." "Take a closer look at it," I responded.

And then it dawned on him. "That's no cloud! It's the glacier on the crater of Kilimanjaro. It doesn't even look real," he murmured. Then he sank into his chair thinking: "It's going to take seven months to get to that peak. What the hell did I agree to come here for?"

Then Diane looked up from the magazine she was reading and asked, "Are you sure, where do you see it?" So Kyle said, "Look over there (pointing to a fixed point through the bus window), now look straight up above the clouds, you can see the snow and ice on the crater rim."

She followed his directions and then she saw the peak hovering above the clouds like a ghostly image. She exclaimed, "Yes, I think I can see it, but I'm not sure I believe my eyes. It's way up there, like it's not even part of this earth." We were on our way to the peak, but the excitement and anticipation gave her butterflies in her stomach.

We arrived in Moshi and the minivans stopped at the Davanu office. We got out and had no idea what would happen next. We looked around and asked the driver: "Now what?" "Zara send car," was his response as he got in the van and took off. We stood in the parking lot and waited. And waited. We waited and after a while we wondered if we'd been ditched in the middle of Africa.

Zara Tanzanian Adventures was the facilitator in Moshi, but we didn't know who "they" were, or if they knew who and where we were. We had already learned that the buses in Africa were not on a schedule like the Swiss trains, but that eventually they came through.

Sure enough, after a while the Zara car showed up, except that it was a tiny subcompact. We shoehorned the gear and ourselves into the car and headed somewhere.

We tried to talk to our driver, but he didn't speak or understand much English, and we know even less Swahili. Each time we spoke to him or asked a question, he would respond with the same sentence, "We see Zainab."

We were glad to hear him put so much faith in Zainab, because she was our only contact in all of Tanzania. I thought about our meeting at the Fairview in Nairobi with Chris and Avril MacDonald of Rafiki Africa.

They had described in some detail that once we arrived in Moshi we would be dealing with Zara. If we needed something or had questions about the mountain or anything in Tanzania, we should simply talk with Zainab Ansell. She is the proprietor of Zara International.

At the Zara office, Zainab came out of her office to meet us. She was dressed in cheerful attire and greeted us with a warm smile. "How are you? Everything okay? Are you tired? We're going to get you settled at your hotel in just a few minutes." She said all of this in one quick breath.

We liked her immediately and Diane was visibly impressed with her. We wondered how she got in this position of business and power in Tanzania. We had already noticed that women are not treated as equals in Kenya or Tanzania.

When dealing with the airport personnel, the government officials, the hotel employees, all the various bus and taxi drivers, Diane was ignored or brushed off. It was very annoying and difficult to deal with. Simple tasks would take longer just because of their attitude toward women.

She had to establish authority before proceeding with the business at hand. We noticed women in the work force, but Zainab was the only business woman we saw who was in any kind of position of power — especially in a superior position over a large number of men.

Zainab growled a few instructions at our driver, changing her tone and facial expression with him as she spoke. He acknowledged her with respect. With us, it was friendly customer service, and with her employees, it was very abrupt business, serious and direct.

She told us that we would be picked up at 8:00 o'clock the next morning. I had seen how positive results come out of this confusion and chaos, and I believed for the first time that this whole disorganization was actually working. With that they whisked us away to the Springland guesthouse.

On our way from the Zara office to the Springland we turned off the city streets, which were paved, but full of pot holes, onto a horrible dirt road, full of ruts and deep holes. We continued bouncing down this dirt road for about fifteen minutes.

The dirt road was lined with small houses and huts. Many were pieced together with sticks and mud. Our presence was acknowledged by unattended dogs, chickens, and goats dodging the treadless tires of our transporter. We continued driving into territory that was more and more abandoned and desolate. No one said anything until Kyle broke the silence and thought out loud, "Is this driver taking us out to the middle of nowhere to rob us?" "Don't be ridiculous," I responded to comfort him, but it did feel a little unsettling.

A few minutes later, the dirt road made a gentle turn to the left and a modern looking building emerged. Once inside the gate of the Springland, Diane was glad to see flowers and grass in the

Zainab, our very capable Tanzania facilitator, and James, our driver in Moshi, with Kyle and Hal.

courtyard. It meant someone cared enough to beautify the place. All the people we met in Moshi seemed friendly with permanent smiles on their faces. They were always willing to help and do anything for us. We were welcomed, chatted with the help, and took a few pictures. Cameras must be rare in East Africa, because many people who had their pictures taken with us asked us to send them copies. We gladly agreed.

As a matter of fact, by the time we had all the pictures developed and had settled back into our middle-class grind at home, Christmas was approaching. We bought inexpensive frames, packaged up a few goodies, and made a Christmas package for them, which we sent to Zainab for distribution to all the kind people. It took four months to arrive!

Zainab sent an e-mail thanking us for the gifts and mentioned that the entire town of Moshi had heard about our "generosity" and how everyone wished they could have had the opportunity to do some work for us. It made us feel good that such a small gesture could generate so much good will.

We saw thousands and thousands of people in Nairobi, Namanga, Arusha, Moshi, and all the other small villages we passed through. One time Kyle blurted out, "Look at that man over there." Diane and I both turned our heads and looked in the direction that Kyle pointed to.

We noticed an obese man. It really had not occurred to us that nobody was overweight until we saw that overweight man in Moshi. It was so unusual, he really stood out. It must be because Kenya and Tanzania are so poor that food is hard to come by, especially fancy foods that are rich in calories. And nobody has a TV, so there are no couch potatoes.

You cannot go to Africa without remembering the children. We saw hordes of little children along the side of the road, playing, walking, and just standing idly outside of their homes. They are wide-eyed and adorable.

Almost all of them smiled and waived at us. They seemed so happy just to see a car or bus go by and when we waived back at them, their smiles became even bigger; sometimes we even coaxed a laugh out of them. They were so cute and lovable, but amazingly poor. They were adorable to meet, but at the same time you had to feel sorry for them in their squalor, and wonder what kind of future they had.

Annie, our hostess at the Springland, showed us to our room, which was clogged with three single beds covered with mosquito nets. Our gear filled the remaining space in the room. It was luxurious in the sense that it had a bathroom.

While getting settled, we organized our gear into specific bags. What we didn't need for Kilimanjaro, we put into a separate bag to be held at the Zara storage facility in Moshi. We re-checked our gear to make sure that we had everything we needed for the mountain.

Our last chance to obtain anything would be in Moshi the next morning. Diane kidded me about spending more time with the gear than with her. But all the gear had to be A-okay, and my job was multiplied by three, because I had inherited the responsibility for everyone's stuff.

After an early dinner, Diane had her eyes on the bathtub in our room, thinking it may be the last opportunity for five or six days to get a decent bath. We forced ourselves to stay awake until a reasonable time, because we did not want to wake up at 1:00 A.M. with nothing to do.

We managed to stay up past 8:00 P.M. before we went to bed. I fell asleep immediately. About two hours later I woke up. At first I lay in bed and tried everything I knew to put myself to

Kilimanjaro Adventure 83

sleep. I tried counting sheep; thinking of nothing; I tried self-hypnosis. About three hours went by like that. It was extremely frustrating. The jet lag was really playing havoc on my internal clock. I had not considered that it would be so severe. I hoped I wouldn't have to embark on the biggest climb of my life with little or no sleep. I wished I had brought some sleeping pills. Of course, I had not, because I didn't use them at home and didn't even think I might need them here. I got up and read a book about an expedition to Aconcagua for a while.

If I couldn't sleep, I might as well get inspired by the expeditions of others or at least sympathize with the miseries they endured. I had just completed reading *Into Thin Air*, by Jon Krakauer, and remembered him talking about climbing with little or no sleep for days. That gave me hope. Okay, so I'm not one of those Himalayan apes climbing Everest, but Kilimanjaro is no molehill either.

Maybe I could be successful on Kilimanjaro with little or no sleep. Just to be safe I was going to resort to a proven antidote created by modern medicine and look for sleeping pills in Moshi the next day. Perhaps some of the other climbers might even have some. Fortunately, the first day on the mountain was supposed to be an easy hike, only about three to four hours.

5

On the Mountain

We got up at about 6:30 A.M. after a terrible night's sleep. An hour and a half later we had eaten, packed up, and were ready to go. As usual, the transportation schedule was ill defined and vague.

Since we were on the edge of town, we simply had to wait. I roamed the courtyard and started talking to a neatly dressed man tending a van in the compound. After a few minutes of small talk, it became apparent that he was our driver, James. We quickly loaded up the van expecting to leave, when James said that he had to pick up four other people and take them to the bus station.

They were the four still eating breakfast, because they thought they would be picked up at 9:30. After standing around a while waiting for them and comtemplating the disorganized transportation schedule, we were finally on our way to drop them off.

As we headed toward the mountain, we stopped to pick up two more climbers, which would give us our first chance to talk to fellow mountaineers. They were nice guys in their mid-twenties, named Ellef and Micke. They were engineering graduate students from the University of Stockholm, performing a feasibility study to bring electrical power to Kasulu. This is a small village in Tanzania that presently is not hooked up to the power grid.

They reminded me of when Diane and I were students, except that we didn't have the good fortune of doing fieldwork in East Africa. "What brought you guys here?" I asked. "When the University was offering field assignments, we jumped on this one so we would have a chance to climb Kilimanjaro. We had hoped to get here for years, but we couldn't come up with the money on our own." "Good deal to combine work with pleasure and have a sponsor for your expedition," I commented.

They only had one small pack each, so I asked, "Where's all your gear?" "We don't have much, we'll rent some from Zainab, and pick up a couple of things on the way," Ellef remarked. "This was the first break from our studies that we've had, but it came up all of a sudden and we didn't have a chance to get everything together."

We stopped at Zainab's storage facility, which was well stocked with somewhat dilapidated gear, and they found almost everything they needed. We loaned them a couple of things, and gave them some of our extra snacks, and they were ready to go.

As far as their climbing abilities, I wasn't sure what to think. They didn't act like climbers and they definitely didn't look like climbers. Ellef had a slight build, and the first impression of Micke was that he was not very athletic. He had narrow shoulders with skinny arms and legs, and seemed a little clumsy on his feet. Because we could relate to them, we had high hopes for them.

Zainab had directed us to a "chemist" who supposedly had sleeping pills. This "chemist" was a small pharmacy with a wide assortment of legitimate looking medication bottles on the shelves. At first, I was skeptical and hesitant, but I figured there was no harm in buying some sleeping pills. If I would actually take them was an entirely different story, and I really didn't believe that I would need them to get some shuteye.

By now it was after 11:00 o'clock. We had been in the minivan for over three hours, and we hadn't gone anywhere. It just amazed me how long it took to get even little things accomplished. Of course, we were getting a little eager after several days of traveling.

We were finally done and on our way to the park entrance, which was another half-hour drive. Along the way we glimpsed the peak once again hovering above the clouds. It was vertical, distant, and almost forbidding.

As we drove through the security gate at the park entrance, Diane exclaimed, "Look how beautiful it is. It's so well groomed, just like a botanical garden." "This is the first time we've seen lush vegetation. Along the entire drive from Nairobi to here it was brown and dusty," I commented. "No actually even when we flew over Namibia and the Kalahari Desert, South Africa, and Zimbabwe it was dry and brown."

She added, "All the plants are so lush and healthy looking. See those trees. Their leaves are such a deep green they almost sparkle." Among the pleasant greenery, a scene resembling a mad house greeted us.

There must have been two hundred men sitting in a terraced field. A group of about twenty converged on our van. James talked to a couple of men and then introduced us to one of them. He was our guide.

His name was Fred Mtui. He looked to be in his late forties, with a lean, chiseled face. His hair was short and carefully trimmed with only a few streaks of gray at the temples. He was physically of small stature, although he had strong looking legs. He was a man of few words. He did not say much to us or to any of the men, just the minimum of information we needed.

At first, the twenty or so men that converged on our van seemed mob-like. It quickly became apparent that it was not just a random mob. There was some undefined structure to the group and it was controlled nonverbally by Fred.

Fred obviously commanded a lot of respect from the crowd of men surrounding us. And most importantly, he chose the porters and assistant guides for our group, which were desirable positions for those men.

Kyle whispered to me, "Do you think this old, out-of-shape, cigarette-smoking weakling can guide us up the mountain?" "Looks can be deceptive," I insisted, "plus, judging by his general presence and his strong legs, he looks like he knows how to get up this mountain." "I doubt this guy could guide us up one of those termite mounds we passed along the side of the road," Kyle continued, "and what are all these other guys doing here? They're swarming around us like bees on honey. We came here to climb the mountain, not to be trampled to death in the parking lot."

And then Diane pulled me aside and whispered in my ear, "This Fred seems kinda' gruff. We're going to spend the next five days with him and he doesn't seem very approachable." I tried to smooth things out, "He's got his hands full right now. He seems competent to me." "I'm already a little nervous about the climb and now I'm concerned about the relationship with our guide," Diane added.

And then she thought, like all the other men in Africa, he's dealing mainly with Hal and he's virtually ignoring Kyle and me. Just another example of the male chauvinism here.

Kilimanjaro Adventure

Mad house at Kilimanjaro National Park Headquarters. Our guide, Fred Mtui, is in center looking at the camera.

The men closest to us waived various types of hiking poles in our direction vying for our attention. Each one of them wanted us to pick his wares for us to rent. Fred asked if we had poles and recommended one per person.

Diane added quickly, "Look, they have all different kinds of hiking poles. I've always wondered about using poles and have wanted to try them. Remember, we saw a lot of people use them in Europe and back home."

"Yeah, I think they'll help with balance and taking a load off our knees, especially on this long trek. What kind do you like?" I asked. "Ellef and Micke picked those large wooden poles and they look pretty nice," she responded. "But those high-tech jobbers are adjustable and much lighter," I said. "Let's get those. This way we can get first-hand experience with the poles. If they really help, we can get some back home," she said, and then thought to herself, I hope they help, because my knees are still bugging me from descending that steep scree field on Baldy. I need all the help I can get.

One of the men offering his poles nosed his way close to us and got a little pushy. Fred quickly barked at him and he retreated instantly. This is when Diane took notice and realized that Fred did have his clients' best interest in mind. This loyalty to the clients became more obvious later in the climb as he became less intense and actually warmed up a little.

We looked at the wares that were being offered and settled on high-tech hiking poles that looked like adjustable ski poles. There were several men offering this style, so we started haggling over the price.

After we settled on a price, the man gave us three poles. I asked how we'd return them to him and he said that there would be no problem, he would be here when we returned. I noticed that the handles had initials carved in them; that was his identification brand. I collapsed our poles to a small size that I could put into one of our bags, which would be portered. I figured that even if we needed the poles, it wouldn't be until higher up on the mountain.

Over the next few days, we noticed that Fred was very effective in dealing with all the people on the mountain, including the assistant guides, porters, and cooks. Also, he quickly assessed the capabilities and conditioning of the climbers from day one, and we considered ourselves lucky to have landed a guide as excellent as Fred.

Shortly after meeting him, I told him, "We're not interested in Gillman's Point. Our goal is to make Uhuru Peak." "Okay, we see," was his only reply, but I knew he stored that information in his mental data banks. Over the next few days, we demonstrated by our attitude and abilities that we were serious about reaching the summit.

Once we resolved the situation with the hiking poles, Fred directed a few men to carry our gear to a spot where it could be safely held. Then Fred led me to an A-frame building where I went through the process of obtaining the climbing permit. Because ours had been prearranged, it was more or less waiting for us. We still needed to stand in different lines, sign the right books, and fill out some more forms. Fred knew the woman on our side of the counter who helped with the paperwork. There was a small crowd of climbers arranging for permits. Several of them were turned away, because the permit limit of fifty had been reached for the day.

Within a few minutes we had the official permit that allowed us to climb the mountain and just as importantly gave us access to the various camps and huts along the way. As we finished the permitting process, I noticed Kyle and Diane eating a bite out of small, white cardboard boxes.

It turned out that a little "goodie" box was provided to all the members of our climbing group that included some fried chicken, an apple, and a couple of crackers. There was still plenty of confusion and more waiting, so we had time to sit down and have a snack before we got started. Also, we picked up a 1:75,000 scale map of Kilimanjaro from a small store across from the permit station.

At the trailhead, Fred was doing some final arranging for porters. It looked like more organized chaos. He was talking to a couple of men with ledgers on the side of the trail who were making entries into those ledgers.

We simply observed and wondered how long until we actually started hiking. It seemed that all we had done for days was to sit on planes, wait in airports, sit on buses and minivans, and just stand around and wait.

But we were getting closer now. At least we were standing at the trailhead in our hiking boots. Groups of climbers surrounded us and everyone seemed excited about finally digging their hiking boots into the muddy trail. We passed the time with small talk, but had not yet met the other people in our immediate climbing group. Ellef and Micke, our friends from the bus ride, were actually in another group.

Absent-mindedly I reviewed several large signs and two prominent plaques at the trailhead. The plaques in particular whet my interest. One commemorates Hans Meyer and the first climb of Kilimanjaro to reach the summit on October 6, 1889.

I had just read about his daring ascent in a book, and here was a bronze plaque staring me in the face, making it seem less abstract than before. The other one commemorates the guides and porters who assisted him during the climb.

I was glad to see them get such prominent recognition for their hard work. Six names are on that plaque:

1. Yohana Lauwo - Guide
2. Jonathan Mtui - Assistant Guide
3. Etia Minja - Porter
4. Toma Masna - Porter
5. Makelio Lyima - Porter
6. Mamba Kowera - Porter

Jonathan Mtui? Could there be a relationship to our guide Fred Mtui? Later in the climb, I asked Fred, "The plaque honored Jonathan Mtui, is there any relation to you?" "Yes, he my great-grandfather. He was foreman in a coffee plantation and worked

Kilimanjaro Adventure

for the British and German colonialists at the last part of the nineteenth century. He also work as porter and guide when the early explorers went higher up the mountain. When Hans Meyer came to Moshi to put his team together for first summit ascent, he got picked."

Jonathan Mtui was selected as an assistant guide because of his skill and demonstrated tenacity on the mountain. No wonder Fred knew the mountain so well and was confident in the procedures and processes.

His family had been here for generations. We later learned that he personally had been up the mountain over 400 times, on all the various routes. Maybe that was a good omen that our bags would arrive at the hut after all.

There was another sign of particular interest to us. It delineated the Marangu Route with the various encampments, estimated climbing times, altitude, and vegetation zones. I took a quick look at it and committed the times to memory.

Mandara hut	3 hours	2700 meters	Forest
Horombo hut	5 hours	3720 meters	Moorland
Kibo hut	5 hours	4703 meters	Alpine Desert
Gillman's Point	5 hours	5685 meters	Alpine Desert
Uhuru Peak	1.5 hours	5895 meters	Ice Cap

There are five different vegetation zones: gaining about 1000 meters each day and ending up on an ice cap at the equator. The elevation gains between camps are much greater than on Everest, where the elevation gains between camps averages about 700 meters.

I said to myself, "Well, this is what we've been preparing for and now we're finally here." It seemed the first leg was an easy three hours, which was definitely a good way to warm up to this baby.

The largest sign was what you might consider a "health warning," probably written by lawyers; it appeared their reach extended all the way to the African mountains. The sign made several points:

1. Hikers attempting to reach the summit should be physically fit.
2. If you should have a sore throat, cold, or breathing problems do not go beyond 3000 meters.
3. Children under 10 years of age are not allowed above 3000 meters.
4. If you have heart or lung problems do not attempt the mountain at all without consulting your doctor.
5. Allow plenty of time for the body to acclimatize by ascending slowly.
6. Do not push yourself to go if your body is exhausted or if you have extreme mountain sickness.
7. Drink 4-5 liters of fluid each day. Water is best, but fruit juices are good supplement.
8. If symptoms of mountain sickness or high altitude disease persist please descend immediately and seek medical treatment. Our rescue team is always on stand-by to render such services at Kibo, Horombo, and Marangu H/Q.
9. Please do not litter the trail. Pack all trash and leave the park as clean as you found it.

As I read the sign, I pondered the implication of these points on our circumstances: Point 1. We had trained hard and felt fit, but it left out our two graduate student friends. Point 2 could have been me; I had still not been able to shake the sniffles. Point 3 we

Kilimanjaro Adventure

did not have to worry about, but did they check IDs at 3000 meters? Point 4 sounded like the standard warning written by lawyers before you do any kind of exercise. Point 5 made sense, but given our schedule, we only had limited time. Point 6 seemed reasonable, but we intended to make the top and if we had to crawl on all fours while we were vomiting, we were going. Point 7 was easy, drink lots of water, although some people substituted beer for water. Point 8 would hopefully not be needed. But I knew from a climb I did a few years before on Popocatepetl how quickly a disaster can happen. Point 9 seemed important, because we had heard and read that the trail and camps were full of litter.

While we stood at the trailhead, just about to start our adventure, Kyle was really getting frustrated, especially with all the guides and porters. "What are they doing?" he wondered out loud. "They just seem to be bickering in Swahili. It doesn't make any sense." "They have to get everything organized," I said. "Like who is responsible for what group and who carries what load." I was getting impatient too, but tried to convey a sense of calm and reason.

Diane kept looking around in the hope of seeing some other teenagers, but her hopes were quickly dashed. There were no other children of any age. The youngest hikers she saw were approximately in their mid twenties.

She said to me, "I think we're the only family and I'm a little concerned about Kyle. Do you think the other families know something we don't and that's why we don't see any children? Do you think it was a mistake to go on such a big expedition with him?" "Not necessarily. So far it's been okay and I think he's having a pretty good time. Let's keep our fingers crossed that it stays that way," I replied, but inside I was a little concerned too.

Hal and Kyle waiting impatiently at the trailhead surrounded by chaos.

Then apparently all the logistical details were resolved and within a few minutes Fred said, "Okay, it time to go and start up the mountain." We gladly complied, although we looked back and saw our bags in disarray among a group of porters.

The porters were mostly young natives dressed in a wide range of attire. A few had boots and jackets, but the majority of them were in dilapidated street shoes, sandals, or even flip-flops. Their clothes were mostly tattered pants and shirts, ranging from T-shirts, to Calvin Klein sweatshirts, to business suit jackets. Most of the pieces were obviously hand-me-downs given to them by previous climbers.

Fred noticed our nervous looks as we started walking up the trail and said, "No problems, it all be there." Hakuna Matata — no problems — seems to be the national slogan. But Fred had

Kilimanjaro Adventure 97

obviously gone through this procedure many times and although at first it appeared chaotic, he organized everything with a certain elegance and respect from the mobs of people around us.

As Kyle turned and looked back, he saw a boy about his age, who picked up two of our bags that had been roped together, and hoisted the load onto his back. That left him speechless and he just thought, "What a shock. I can't imagine lugging big heavy loads up Kilimanjaro to earn some money. These kids must be doing it so they can survive. That does give me a whole new appreciation for the American way of life, and respect for these porters."

So we were finally on the trail. The trail started out wide, the equivalent of a nearly one-lane dirt road, but it quickly narrowed down as we ascended. The scenery was dense forest, almost pure jungle.

There were tall trees and in places plants were growing on other plants. Plants that if you wanted to buy them at a nursery in the U.S. would cost you a pretty penny. Within a few more minutes the trail narrowed further to a footpath.

Up ahead, a couple of hikers had stopped. They were looking in the bushes on the side of the trail. It piqued our curiosity, especially when they waved to us and said, "You've got to come and see this." We picked up our pace until we caught up with them. We turned and peered into the dark foliage where we saw a troop of big monkeys in the bushes. They were Blue monkeys, eating some unidentifiable fruit.

We scooted closer to take some flash pictures, which didn't seem to bother them the least. They were probably used to hikers. This was the first time in all the years of hiking and mountain climbing we had come across wild monkeys on the trail. The jungle was dense and formed a shielding canopy that protected us from the searing rays of the sun. The whole setting, especially with the monkeys, evoked the spirit of Edgar Rice Burroughs' *Tarzan of the Apes* stories.

Full of energy at the beginning of a long hike. Left to right: Ellef, Micke, Diane, Fred, and Kyle.

Further up the trail another hiker had stopped. He had a young Jackson's chameleon on his finger. We took pictures and were amazed by all the exotic flora and fauna. Contrary to expectations, there were no pesky insects and spiders on the mountain and the numerous bottles of insect repellent that we had brought happily remained unused.

As we progressed along the trail, we crossed several small, rickety wooden bridges, which added more character than substance to the trail. Almost in every case, the narrow ravines they spanned could have been traversed with little effort without the bridges. The trail was wet and slippery at times. In some places, it was muddy and there were standing puddles of water. I asked Fred, "If the trail is this wet, it must have rained recently. Does it rain a lot here?"

"It rain almost every day, summer or winter, and pour heavy during rain season. Last month, we hiked through here and it rain real hard. Everybody in my group got real wet. The clothes never dried, and they didn't have enough dry clothes. By the time we reach Horombo camp, everybody was freezing cold. We had to turn around and go back down. Do you have dry clothes?" he asked.

"Yes, we brought extra clothes and they're sealed in a large plastic bag," I replied. "In case it rains they won't get wet. I don't want a little rain to stop us." He just nodded, realizing we did our best to be prepared.

Kyle and Diane were so far ahead of me by now that I couldn't even see them. Generally, I was the first one up the mountain, but I saw no reason to go fast on this leg of the climb. I knew I was still going faster than I should have been. I could feel it in my legs, and because of the hot and humid weather in this altitude zone, I was sweating considerably, but I didn't want to fall too far behind.

Diane set a comfortable pace for herself, which was unusually quick and allowed her to enjoy the forested trail by herself. Parts of the trail reminded her of the Naulu trail we had hiked on Hawaii a couple of weeks before.

While on Hawaii we not only climbed Mauna Kea for altitude training, but we also hiked in Volcano National Park. At that time the Puuoo Cone of the Kilauea Volcano was erupting and spewing red-hot lava high into the brilliant sky. To get a good vantage point we had to hike about two hours over an undulating, black lava field and then another hour and a half through a tropical forest. The trail was encroached on by the heavy growth and the ground was carpeted in moss and ferns.

Marangu trail winds through dense forest at lower altitude.

It was a spectacular trail and well worth the hike. The red lava fountain that emerged from deep within the volcano was a spellbinding sight. We knew we would not see flowing lava on Kilimanjaro, but the lush trail was equally as beautiful as that Naulu trail.

The trail had narrowed to a thin line of dirt in the forest with roots and fresh growth infringing on the muddy path. The vegetation around the trail changed gradually from dense forest to thinner, bush-like trees with wisps of moss on them. These were giant heathers, Erica arborea.

Up ahead I thought I saw Kyle around one of the bends. After several switchbacks I caught up with him and noticed that he was working pretty hard. I told him, "Pole, pole (pronounced polay)." That's Swahili for slow, which is what some of the porters said to us as we passed them. For the next twenty or thirty minutes we hiked together and talked about how beautiful and exotic the trail was.

We continued talking about stuff. Nothing in particular, just guy stuff. We hardly talked to each other at home, but here we were having a wonderful conversation. It was almost as if he had to let down his defenses, so meticulously crafted during his teenage years.

Now that we were finally on the mountain, Diane was getting caught up in the hike and no longer intimidated by its size. She felt ready for the challenge and was set on going as high as she could.

Near the camp, her ankle started bothering her. It began to tighten up and throb. She was a little worried that it was giving her a problem after the first day's hike. This did not bode well for the rest of the climb, but she kept it to herself for now.

Through the vegetation, we saw there was some type of ridge ahead, maybe the Mandara encampment. A couple more switchbacks confirmed there were huts. The first three-hour section took us two hours. Diane actually finished ahead of us by several minutes.

There was only a handful of hikers in the camp when we emerged from the dense brush. We sat in a large grassy field and cooled off from the strenuous hike through the jungle. Other climbers slowly trickled into camp, but it took almost an hour longer for the gear to arrive. The porters knew to take it slow and steady with their heavy loads.

Relaxing at Mandara camp after the first day's hike.

Our quick pace probably reflected the pent-up energy and the joy of finally getting on the mountain. And also the competitive nature of climbers is to show each other how fast or how radical an ascent can be performed.

Since our ascent was anything but radical, we had to show off with speed. I didn't see any need for it at that time, especially this early in the hike. But in a sense it was good, because we would recover quickly and it would help build "mountain legs" — legs that were used to climbing uphill.

The Mandara encampment sits in a jungle clearing on a gently sloped, grassy field. It consists of a main mess hall surrounded by about eight or ten small huts for the hikers. A short distance away is another six or eight small huts for porters, and one hut called the "reception." This is a small "store" where you can buy water, drinks, and a few supplies.

We all crashed on the grass and waited while Fred arranged for our huts. The huts are small, but clean and comfortable. There are four cots per hut with a clean foam mattress and a small pillow. The loads of gear filled the rest of the space in the small hut.

Kyle resting comfortably in the hut at Mandara camp.

This was pure luxury compared to pitching tents and camping. Even though on the Machame and other routes, where there are fewer permanet camps, the climbers don't exactly "rough it" either. Oh those routes, the porters carry the gear and tents, and then set up camp while the climbers relax. So what it really means is that the porters have more work and you sleep closer to the ground. As we claimed our bunks in the hut, a personable young woman poked her head in the narrow door. "I guess we'll be bunkmates for the next few days," she remarked in a cheerful Australian accent as she occupied the bunk next to Diane's. She introduced herself as Michelle and was part of our climbing group, guided by Fred. She was young, mid to late twenties, and was traveling by herself through East Africa.

We immediately compared notes on difficult climbs we had performed and discussed the strategic differences between rugby and football. She had little experience with high altitude, but had always wanted to experience Africa and Kilimanjaro. We thought it was gutsy of her to travel to these parts alone.

Our porters fixed tea and served biscuits. The climbers had time to sit and talk. Some chose to read or write in their journals, go for short walks, or just relax. It was a very pleasant way to enjoy the camp.

One of the nearby trees came alive with the chatter and commotion of a group of monkeys. Kyle and I rushed over to get a closer view. They were Colobus monkeys, about ten or twelve, including two females with small babies. They were strikingly beautiful animals with shiny black fur and a long cape of white hair on their backs that extends into a flowing white tail. The white capes on their backs caught air and ballooned up like a sail when they jumped between branches or trees.

It was a joy to see those spectacular Colobus monkeys in a nearby tree put on a show for us. There was nothing like it in a zoo, even at our world famous San Diego Zoo or Wild Animal Park. Although the zoos have the same species, there is no comparison to seeing them frolic in the wild.

Kyle and I talked as we watched the monkeys. We communicated like good friends, not like the disciplinarian and the rebellious teenager, which was our normal mode of interacting. I also observed him talking to other climbers. He was the only teenager around and many of the adults enjoyed talking to him and included him in their conversations to get a young person's perspective. We were learning a lot about him and it was such a pleasure that we didn't have to inflict our usual parental duties on him. He was not the irresponsible teenager we thought he was before the trip. He was actually turning into a young adult right before our eyes.

The porters fixed dinner and served it in the mess hall. There were several plates of potatoes, spaghetti, cooked carrots, and some type of meat that could have been beef. It was all edible and some of it actually tasted good. After dinner there was more coffee and tea and a short description of the plans for the next day: wake-up call at 7:00, breakfast at 7:30, hit the trail by 8:00.

On the bus ride from Nairobi to Moshi, we had already learned that the concept of time, and a schedule, was different in Africa than in the United States; we would have to see what these plans translated to in African time.

While there was still some light, we arranged the sleeping gear, the packs, and the hut, and headed back to the mess hall. There, we socialized and played cards, while Kyle read next to us in the dim artificial light. There was limited electricity provided by photovoltaic solar panels and a large bank of lead acid batteries. It had been a great first day on the mountain.

The after-dinner conversation had moved out onto the deck of the mess hall and proceeded in a lively manner. There was a boisterous group of South Africans having a rousing party. They were a bunch of medical doctors and some had brought their wives. In addition to their guide and porters, they had hired an expedition leader named Allen.

Allen, about forty, was dapper in his Dallas Cowboys jacket. According to Diane, he was a ruggedly handsome man, with an athletic build. It was Allen's third tour of Kilimanjaro and he had summited Uhuru Peak the previous two times.

Beer and whiskey were flowing freely among this group and some were smoking pipes and cigars. We were wondering about this scene, so Diane asked Allen, "You're drinking beer and alcohol on the mountain; aren't you worried about any ill effects with the altitude?" "We're drinking at this camp, but after this we'll get serious. No more alcohol," he replied. We wondered if his group knew about the rule, because they looked like they really knew how to party.

6

Getting Higher

We were dog-tired from the jet lag, but struggled to keep ourselves awake until past 8:00 P.M. Once we retired, we fell asleep immediately. Around 11 o'clock I woke up frustrated by that sinking feeling of another sleepless night. I certainly didn't want to stare at the dark ceiling all night long again. I fidgeted in bed for about an hour, unable to go back to sleep and wrestled with the idea of the sleeping pills.

Was that "chemist" a legitimate pharmacist or some type of village witch doctor? Would the pills make me sick or have some harmful side effects, especially because some medications affect a person differently at altitude? I thought, what the hell, anything's better than another night without sleep, and with that I took two pills and slowly faded away.

The next time I woke up it was still dark and I noticed Diane in the cot next to mine checking the time on her luminous dial watch. I asked timidly, "Do I want to know what time it is?"

"Sure. It's 6 A.M.," she answered. Yes — I had slept all night, and there were no unpleasant side effects from the pills. Kyle and she had slept fairly well, not quite through the night, but they weren't ready to resort to medication yet.

We had a big breakfast of hot chocolate, tea, porridge, bread, boiled eggs, and the tiniest bananas we've ever seen. And best of all, my sinuses had cleared up; maybe my sniffles were not a cold, but just an irritation from contaminated air.

The air on the mountain was crystal clear and even had a distinctly clean scent to it. After breakfast, we dug out our stash of vitamin tablets, and we each took a small handful.

Congregating in the morning for the next leg of the climb.

We gathered in camp, which had a slight mist hanging over it from the cool morning air. We were ready to leave and it was about 8:30 A.M. Pretty good timing, considering the guides had the

Kilimanjaro Adventure

formidable job of herding a bunch of disorganized climbers. There were several large groups and all started on the trail one after the other.

The trail was jammed with people. There must have been over fifty, counting climbers, guides and porters. Fortunately, this congestion lasted for only about ten minutes before it dissipated. That was the first time the trail was crowded or congested. As a matter of fact, it was the only time.

We had heard how crowded this route was, but in reality, we had the trail to ourselves most of the time. Or we chose the people we wanted to hike with. In that respect, it was very pleasant.

At the camps, there were groups of people, especially in the mess halls. This allowed for social intercourse and added to the enjoyment of sharing mountain climbing experiences and other lighthearted discussions. Heavy-duty political discussions were adeptly avoided.

Some groups turned off the main trail to view the nearby Maundi Crater and others spread out due to different rates of hiking. Kyle just kind of snickered, "Maundi Crater, what's that all about. We didn't come all this way to look at some Podunk crater." "We came here to look at the real crater," I chimed in. "Yeah, the one we saw from the plane, that punctured the clouds," he added. "The one we saw from the road that looked like it was part of the sky." "The big K. It's that or nothing!" We all agreed.

So we bypassed the crater and after about a half an hour the forest subsided. The terrain opened up to the moorland and a small plateau surrounded by a field of flowering shrubs and bushes. That was the first time that we got a nice view of Mawenzi, the secondary peak of Kilimanjaro. It was a beautiful setting and the majority of hikers took the pleasant scenery as an excuse for the first break. We felt that we had just started and didn't want to interrupt our momentum, so we continued without Fred, or anyone else. We were rewarded by a beautiful view of both Kibo and Mawenzi just a short time later.

View of Kibo and Mawenzi from the lower moorland zone.

Kibo, which is the primary peak of Kilimanjaro, was still far away, but it didn't look as massive and impossible to reach as in all our previous sightings. Diane was happy to be on this part of the trail, especially when she saw us getting closer to the dormant crater.

She said, "When I look at the snow-covered crater now it doesn't scare me as much. Not like when we first saw it out the window from the airplane." "We're slowly putting a dent in this mountain," I observed. "I still don't know about getting up that immense scree field," she confided in me. "The best thing is to put it out of your mind and when we get there you'll do just fine," I reassured her.

The weather was perfect — sunny and warm with a brilliant blue sky. We were above the cloud layer, which hovered over the valleys below. By now the vegetation had changed to low shrubs, mostly heath bushes interspersed with flowering bushes and grasses. In addition to electrifying yellow and orange blossoms, there were seas of blue and purple buds.

As the day progressed, some thin clouds gathered imperceptibly above us, which made hiking in the moorland pleasant and prevented the equatorial sun from beating down on us. We applied sun screen and lip balm liberally, especially as we ascended, because the ultra-violet rays get very intense with altitude. We still got a great view of the surroundings. The terrain was rolling hills with several large valleys and ridges, covered with flowering grass and bushes.

This part of the trail had deep furrows carved out by heavy downpours that soak the mountain in rainy seasons. These furrows extended along the trail for long distances and resembled the gutters in a bowling alley, except that they were two to three times as deep and hundreds of times longer.

Kyle envisioned rolling a bowling ball down one of those furrows and wondered how long it would go before it finally jumped the confining trench. Later he told me that he played these mind games to keep from "losing it" completely.

We were hiking at a comfortable pace over gently rolling hills for several hours without a break. A prominent ridge ahead of us looked like it would make a good place to rest. We took a short break, had a little lunch, and continued our comfortable pace. Our pace was slow, but we were ahead of all the other climbers. The three of us had the trail to ourselves. There was nobody around, except occasionally we hiked past porters who were taking a break on the side of the trail.

Porters making their way through the moorland with heavy loads.

We enjoyed hiking and talking as a group. Kyle was leading at one time when he turned around and said, "I'm having a great time. How about you guys?" "Yeah, this is fabulous," was Diane's response. It was fabulous, but the most amazing thing was that our teenager admitted to having a good time with his parents. This was more than we had expected and if nothing else made the whole trip worthwhile.

However, I became somewhat concerned about Diane's ankle due to the long hike over rocky terrain. While training for this climb it had occasionally flared up and didn't have a chance to heal completely. We were covering a lot of ground and we still had the major climbing ahead of us. She didn't let on that there was a problem, so I put it out of my mind.

An important benefit of these long treks is that it removes all the nagging little concerns that normally clutter the mind. This frees the mind to develop new ideas and tackle problems that otherwise receive little or no attention.

That is what happened to me on this part of the trail. I had just started a new project at work — a solar-powered rocket stage. We had been struggling with a particular issue regarding the transfer of concentrated solar power to a high-temperature thermal storage device. I kept going over the issue from all angles until I developed a workable solution. At the break, I recorded my ideas on paper for testing back home. It turned out to be a good idea that advanced the project.

We continued hiking up and down brush-covered ridges. We passed a unique kind of plant, a cross between a cactus and a tree, called Giant Senecios, Senecio kilimanjari. This species is found only on Kilimanjaro. Kyle and I were studying the hills and ridges and discussing which one would be the last one before the Horombo camp would be visible.

It's frequently difficult to tell the relative heights of peaks and ridges in the mountains, because the terrain can throw off your perception. I kept checking the altitude; my altimeter was reading about 3600 meters.

Kyle was eager to reach the next camp and started to pull away. He came up to the ridge that we had predicted would be the last one, desperately hoping not to see another valley. Before he rounded the last switchback, he could smell the aroma of food cooking on an open fire, which brought a big smile to his face.

The compound was already teaming with activity from the porters. The layout of the structures was similar to the Mandara

A cluster of Giant Senecios.

camp with a main mess hall, numerous huts and separate quarters for the porters and guides. But now we were above timberline and the only plants were some low bushes and scrub scattered among the volcanic sand. We had ascended into the clouds, which gave the camp an austere feeling.

We had heard stories about how much litter was on the trail and in the camps because of the ever-increasing hordes of people on the mountain. Supposedly, almost ten thousand people a year attempt to climb Kilimanjaro now, the majority of them on the trail we were using. However, we were pleasantly surprised to see how clean the mountain was.

The trail and the camps were free of litter and were remarkably clean and tidy. We saw more discarded water bottles and candy wrappers when we hiked back home in the local mountains than we did here. The Tanzanian National Park is responsible for the condition of the facilities and services including the trails, huts, guides, porters, and rescue. We have to give them credit for cleaning up the mountain and making it accessible to large numbers of climbers. They are doing a fine job.

Second leg of climb is complete at the Horombo camp.

There was an international assortment of people on the mountain. More than half were European, mostly from Germany, Spain, England, France, and the Scandinavian countries. This large European contingent can be explained by their interest in mountains and the short four- or five-hour flight from most European cities to Nairobi or Kilimanjaro International Airport. However, we also encountered South Africans and Australians, but not too many Americans.

Americans were in a minority, perhaps less than twenty percent. But most people spoke English, including the guides and proprietors of the "reception." There was also a wide range of athletic abilities and personalities present. The majority of people basically looked "fit." But some looked strong and ready to climb a big mountain, while others looked feeble and didn't give the impression of being able to reach the top.

Allen, sporting a big smile and a bottle of Safari Lager beer, cheerfully greeted us when we first arrived at Horombo. We asked him about his group, and he said, "I instructed them to visit the Maundi crater and to really take their time to reach Horombo camp. I told them not to arrive at Horombo before 3:00 o'clock." He had hiked quickly to Horombo to reserve some good huts for his group, because they were going to stay an extra day to acclimatize.

The rest of our gear arrived and Fred said, "I sorry to tell you, but your bunks are above the mess hall." That was probably the worst location, because there were about twenty bunks in the busiest hut of the camp. However, the smaller, more private huts were reserved for the groups who spent the extra day on the mountain for acclimatizing.

After we grabbed three bunks, we went downstairs for hot tea and cocoa, and some hot roasted peanuts. It was amazing how good everything tasted on the mountain. We sat around, talked, or read and wrote. However, a number of people were starting to have trouble with the altitude.

They were uncomfortable, with headaches, nausea, and vomiting. Our graduate student friend, Micke, was huddled by himself, looking pale to a light shade of green. He had been vomiting earlier, but it seemed to have subsided for a while.

Ellef and he planned on staying an extra day at Horombo to rest and for acclimatizing. The way things were going for them it looked like they needed it. The three of us were feeling no different than at sea level. But we would have to see how we would feel once we got past the Kibo hut.

I asked Fred, "We're running low on drinking water. Where's the best place to get more?" "All the running water from outdoor faucets is safe to drink," he responded. "There no reason to buy bottled water, it too expensive at the reception this high on mountain." I had also heard that much of the bottled water was collected at this altitude and sold as fresh mountain water without further purification.

I believe Fred knew what he was talking about, but being the paranoid American that I am, I filled our bottles and added iodine tablets just to be extra safe. To top it off, I mixed in some packets of powdered Gatorade for energy and flavor.

Kyle came out of the hut with his book and announced, "That Dutch guy is up in our room blowing chunks all over the place." "Poor guy, I hope he's all right," Diane commented. "Yeah, I hope he gets better soon, " I added, "because we have to sleep up there."

We felt sorry for those not doing well. However, we were going to need a good night's sleep since we would only have three or four hours rest at Kibo hut the next night, before making our summit attempt. Oh well, we'd managed well so far; I hoped that we could keep it up.

Diane, Kyle, and I were feeling spectacularly well, we laughed and shared funny stories. People were watching us and noticed how energetic we were, as well as the camaraderie between us. They asked us what our secret was. There really was none, except that we had tried to train at altitude as much as possible and kept ourselves well hydrated. We had worked a long time to get here and we were enjoying it to the fullest.

The clouds completely obscured the views to the valley, and it was getting darker. By now, it was after 4:00 P.M. and Allen was on his third Safari Lager (but who was counting?). There was still no sign of his group. He occasionally chatted with us, showing some signs of anxiousness and preoccupation watching for his entourage.

About an hour later they arrived and the partying started again. They had a large supply of mixed drinks, commercially available in Johannesburg. These were contained in small packets, similar to ketchup or mustard packets, just larger. They looked like they were designed for smuggling into ball games or concerts where alcohol is not allowed.

We found their alcohol consumption really surprising. We shared stories of the day's hike and asked some of the doctors how they were feeling. They told us that they had brought a lot of medication with them and were prepared to treat themselves as needed: one of the privileges of being a doctor. Fred thought they would have trouble higher up because of the drinking. Of course, he was right.

However, the doctors were not just partying; they did offer professional advice. At one time, two of them had isolated Micke and they were treating him for altitude sickness. They gave him heavy doses of Diamox (acetozolomide) to help him metabolize more oxygen.

They talked about whether Micke should descend. Since Micke responded well to the medication and treatment, and was resting comfortably, they decided to wait and evaluate him after twenty-four hours at Horombo.

One of the doctors was talking to Kyle and they seemed to have a good conversation going. Later in the conversation, he asked Kyle, "Did you want to come here, or did your Dad force you to?" "No, my parents left it up to me and I decided it was a great idea," Kyle responded. "Do you do a lot of mountain climbing back home?" "Well, I used to, but I haven't for a few years." "Then you know that the air gets real thin up there and you need strong lungs and a high red blood cell count to be able to make it," he continued. "Do you think you have what it takes?" Kyle was taken aback, but lacked the finesse to rebut him.

Kyle couldn't believe the doctor was questioning his ability to climb the mountain, especially when the man didn't even know anything about him. Kyle changed his opinion of the doctor and thought he was a jerk.

He wanted to let him know, but out of respect, he simply said, "I've done well in the past, and so far I'm not having any problems, so I think I'll be okay." Kyle let it go with that, but took it as a challenge, which really fired him up and made him more determined than ever to reach the summit.

As the three of us were talking before dinner, Kyle complained, "It would be great to have some canned, chunky soup." To which I replied: "I don't have soup, but I brought a couple of cans of pork and beans." He got all excited and said, "Let's find Fred to see if he can warm them up for us."

We finally located him in one of the smaller huts, where the porters were cooking over a small fire in the middle of the hut. It was smoke filled and the guides and porters were sitting in the thick smoke carrying on and being merry. Fred said, "No problem."

The meal was good, consisting of rice, cooked carrots, overcooked potatoes, and chicken, and the three of us shared the baked beans. All the food was good, but the beans provided a real treat.

A taste of home. This small matter changed the entire atmosphere of dinner. Kyle was energized and wished we had brought ten cans of beans. The others at the table asked about the beans. Kyle explained how at home he cooked them with cheese, onions, or hot dog slices. It was a real pleasure to see how much he enjoyed those beans and how for a while he led the conversation at the dinner table.

Dinner was late that night so we immediately headed up to our bunks. Kyle had a bottom bunk and was reading a book by the dim light of his headlamp, when he heard a scratching noise near the wall. He looked up and in the beam of the headlamp, there was a large mouse, the size of a rat, with a big long tail, staring right at him. He just about chased the varmint out of the building.

Not that the sight of a mouse frightened him, but because of all the vaccinations we received, he was thinking about the strange diseases that lingered in Africa. The rest of the night he kept himself bundled up to prevent an attack by any disease-infested mice.

After what seemed like a short night, two Spaniards from the climbing group that included Ellef and Micke were up at 5:00 A.M. They intended to hike past Kibo hut for additional acclimatization. Their departure was noisy, and soon after the porters started setting the tables below in the mess hall.

That meant our night was over. After breakfast we packed up our gear and were ready for the next leg. Some of the climbers stood around and talked. Since many of them were staying at the camp for another day of acclimatization, there were words of encouragement and a friendly atmosphere permeated the camp. Meeting other climbers and swapping stories and experiences are always wonderful parts of any climb.

Kilimanjaro Adventure

We set out on the trail and, unlike the two previous days, we stayed in a fairly tight group of seven: the three of us, a German couple named Uschi and Gerd, Michelle, and Fred. Those six people were Fred's climbing group. It was the first time we were all together. There was no illusion of climbing teams, just groups of people. On a team you are dependent on the skills and cooperation of others and they on you, while in a group you are simply with others, but you don't work together toward a common goal. Given the nontechnical nature of the climb, there was no need to have teams anyway.

About a half hour into the hike, Michelle reached into her pack for her camera. She wanted to take a picture and quickly realized that she didn't have her camera. Then she remembered that she had inadvertently left it on a rock, back at the Horombo camp where she had taken a picture that morning. She decided to go back and look for it.

Fred was irritated, because he told everyone early on to watch out for personal items. Especially at the camps, because there were a lot of people and things could disappear. We continued without her and she would catch up with us later. As it turned out, her trip back to the camp was in vain, and she never saw the camera again.

We crossed an unassuming ravine that was dissected with shallow channels filled with icy, glacial run off and covered with a low, hardy vegetation. A horizontal pipe captured some of the cold, clear water on the uphill side, which trickled out the open end. An important sign dangled from the pipe that read "Last Water," which encouraged us to stop and fill our containers.

The trail meandered through a few more small ridges with less and less vegetation. Soon we had a beautiful view of Mawenzi.

It 's very jagged and looked difficult to climb. Fred said few people attempt it, because it's very technical. In addition, it is Kibo's little brother and therefore has less attraction for casual climbers, but it is the third highest peak in Africa, after Kibo and Mount Kenya.

The Kibo cone rising out of the upper moorland with Fred, Diane, Kyle, and Hal in foreground.

A few ridges later, the vegetation thinned and we gazed across the expanse of a vast plain known as the Saddle. This was a high desert region flooded with sunshine. It was almost devoid of any plant or animal life and was mostly volcanic sand, freckled with large rocks and boulders.

The air was crisp and clear, which made for an extensive view and deceptive distances. The crater pyramid soared majestically into the clear blue sky. Everything looked closer than it was. Because of the clear air, one can make out more detail and it gives the false impression of closeness. It was breathtaking to see such a wide-open vista high in the mountains.

Kyle overlooking the saddle with Kibo on left and the West Lava Hill on right.

Fred was telling us about some events from other climbs: "This same time last year we hike through here and the weather got bad. It rained and hailed. There no shelter here. We turned back and went to Zebra Rock for shelter. Wait three hours, then went back to Horombo. Wait at Horombo two days, but weather didn't get better. Couldn't go up, so we had to turn around and go down." "The weather looks so perfect right now, I guess we're lucky," was my reply. "This good time to be up here. Weather should be good for a while."

"Fred, tell us more; have you ever had severe problems?" "Sure, about ten people die every year. Last year, a doctor from

America want to reach summit. He push too hard up the Western Breach. In the night he had problems breathing and died in tent. Another time we were near rim on scree field above Kibo hut, when a young man from Norway pulled on a boulder and it rolled on top of him. He and the boulder rolled down the hill and broke his neck." We just listened to all his stories, and then I told him about the screamer I took on Popo.

Our group marched at a slow pace in the meager air, a pace dictated by Fred for our bodies to adapt to the altitude. We met the two Spaniards, who were returning to Horombo. They had hiked past the Kibo hut, part way up the scree field. We had to admire them for exerting so much energy for acclimatizing. I would have been tempted to continue to the summit.

Diane was chatting with Fred and asked him, "Do you have

Kyle, Diane, Gerd, Uschi, and Fred trekking through the Saddle with the jagged peaks of Mawenzi in the background.

any kids?" "I have two sons, they both in their twenties." "Oh, are they porters or guides?" "No, this good job for me, but it tough way to earn money. My sons learn a craft. One training to be a carpenter, the other a mechanic. That not as much hard work."

In talking with Uschi and Gerd we learned that they were on a mission from the Lutheran Church to inspect what had become of the contributions their church had made to a village in Tanzania over the last ten years.

When they landed in the village, they found little progress and lots of excuses. One particular item was about some rain gutters the village had desperately requested about two years ago. The rain gutters were an important means of collecting fresh water, because the village has no running water.

At first, there were no rain gutters to be found anywhere. But then days later, they were shown some that were stuck behind

Foreboding look toward eastern edge of Kibo.

the church, which had obviously been put there for their benefit. Uschi fully expected them to be removed, and not installed, once they left. As part of their trip to Africa, they took a side trip to enjoy Kilimanjaro. This turned out to be more successful than their church mission.

We stopped for a well-deserved rest behind some giant rocks toward the upper part of the Saddle. Even though the sun was shining, it was cold, especially when the wind was blowing. After the rest, we hiked for a short time and when we rounded a ridge, we could see the Kibo hut. It took us five hours from Horombo, which was just right. We purposely went slowly to conserve our strength for the next day.

The Kibo hut is simple, almost crude. It's a single building made from stones gathered from the immediate vicinity and cemented into walls. It's perched on a small, level lot surrounded by

Diane posing in front of Kibo hut.

volcanic sand and rocks, and absolutely no vegetation. It looked as sterile as a moonscape and cast a shadow of anxiety over the climbers.

We rested on some lava boulders while we waited for space to open in the hut. The sun was shining and there was a slight breeze. A young porter came out and said: "I bring you hot tea, biscuits, and popcorn."

We all had a good appetite except Uschi, who was fatigued and afflicted with a severe headache. She wanted to sleep on the rocks, but Fred told her, "No. You better walk it off instead."

We had a fabulous view of the Kibo cone, which loomed ominously behind the hut. We were starting to put a serious dent into the mountain. Just overhead, we could see distinctive parts of the southern glacier field gleaming a light blue in the equatorial sun.

Edge of southern icefield as seen from Kibo hut.

We studied the rest of the terrain and the trail ahead. The first part was a wide path of scree with no defined trail and about a twenty-five to thirty percent grade.

This led to a small ledge, where the Hans Meyer Cave is located. From there the scree field narrowed and from this angle looked almost vertical. It reminded me of looking up at the Trans America building in San Francisco. This is the tall skyscraper that is shaped like a pyramid, so the walls are not quite vertical, but slanted a little.

We had to strain our neck muscles just to look up to the top of the crater rim. We could make out the regular switchbacks again. It looked challenging, but doable. Even with binoculars, we couldn't make out any climbers on the trail; apparently it was too late in the day for climbers to still be on that part of the trail.

Then our rooms became available and we saw the interior of the Kibo hut for the first time. The large stone building consisted of about six unheated rooms, each with ten bunk beds, a central table, and no privacy. It was by far the most primitive lodging conditions on the trail, but nobody was complaining.

The bunks were clean and comfortable and we had a roof over our heads, in case it started to rain or snow. Two smaller buildings were nearby for the guides and porters.

The number of people at this hut had diminished greatly compared to the previous ones, probably due to significant numbers of climbers turning back due to altitude problems and lack of motivation. There is a certain amount of discomfort that goes along with being high in the mountains, and one must want to reach the summit badly enough to accept it.

The first real problem is loss of appetite or simply the inability to eat and digest food. Your body is telling you that food is not compatible with the lack of oxygen at high altitude. Not eating compounds the problem and you get weak and start feeding on your reserves. As city folks, we have plenty of reserves, but for some reason the body starts consuming muscles as well as stored fat. The longer you stay at altitude the worse the problem gets and your body starts to wither away. Nevertheless, we were doing fine and were in good spirits.

After we got our bunk assignments, we settled in and readied our clothing and gear. In addition to Michele, Uschi, and Gerd, we met our newest bunkmates and swapped stories. They were three guys from California named Gary, Shell, and Randy.

Gary was a high school teacher from Los Angeles; Shell a salesman, married three times, who apparently wanted to get away for a while; and Randy who was in the Peace Corps, working in other parts of Africa.

They had hooked up together while on safari before climbing Kilimanjaro. They were real comedians and kept us entertained. More importantly, they distracted everyone from the nervous anticipation of the last leg of the climb.

Fred came in with the instructions for the next day, "We wake you up around midnight. I stay with family. I have Macuba and Kennedy for you and you," gesturing separately at Uschi, Gerd, and Michelle and informing them who their guides would be for the next day. We were glad Fred was with us. From the beginning of the hike, we had made it clear to Fred that we intended to go to Uhuru Peak and nothing less.

On the trail from Horombo to Kibo, Diane nervously asked Fred, "How tough is the steep scree field and how long and hard is it from Gillman's to Uhuru Peak?" And she followed it with a series of other questions.

He answered all her questions one by one, and then summed

it all up with one last statement that stayed with her. He said, "You strong family, you go to Uhuru Peak." That made her feel good and reduced the anxiety about the summit attempt.

We crawled into our sleeping bags at about 7:00 P.M., because we were expecting a midnight wake-up call. The reason for the early start was two-fold.

First, we wanted to take advantage of the cool air for the hardest part of the climb. Second, we didn't know how long it would take to reach the summit and return, and we had to give ourselves as much time as possible. It is especially important to have daylight for the descent, which is frequently the most dangerous part of the climb.

Also, if there was an emergency and a rescue team had to be summoned to assist, we would need all the valuable daylight we could get. The darkness also had the side benefit of not having the long scree field staring us in the face the entire time we were crawling toward the top at a snail's pace.

All the nights on the mountain were cool, but especially at the Kibo hut, it was freezing cold. We had inexpensive zero-degrees Celsius sleeping bags that were comfortable, but not made for arctic conditions. Diane put on her thermal underwear, a pullover, two pairs of socks, and bundled up in her sleeping bag.

She noticed when I got ready for bed, I stripped to my underwear and slipped into my sleeping bag. And then, to top it off, I took those off and tossed them out.

Diane couldn't believe her eyes and wondered how I was able to generate enough body heat to stay warm. She asked, "Aren't you cold? I'm freezing and I'm wearing two layers of clothes." "No I'm not cold. I'm more comfortable this way, so I'll sleep better."

For Diane the temperature didn't really matter; her nerves

kept her too rattled to pretend to sleep anyway. The next day's climb was weighing heavily on her mind. All night long, she heard people tossing and turning. She finally shivered herself to some well-deserved sleep only to be awakened by heavy duty snoring right next to her ear.

As early as 11:00 P.M. she heard guides waking up their clients. As she lay there listening to climbers getting summoned by their guides, she thought, this must be what it feels like to be on death row — waiting to be taken to meet your maker.

7

Summit Day

Shortly after midnight, there was commotion in our room and I quickly emerged from unconsciousness. "Time for final march," I heard Fred say. Gary was already putting his long johns on while he was scolding Shell, "Damn it Shell, I hardly slept at all with you snoring all night."

I didn't remember anyone snoring. And then Kyle leaned close to me and announced, "Dad you snored so loud, I was worried that the ice fields above us of would collapse and come roaring down into the hut in a giant avalanche." I guess it had been me, not Shell, who had been snoring. So I took Shell off the hook, "I was just informed that I was the one who snored. Sorry you guys didn't sleep as well as I did."

The porters served breakfast on the small table in the center of our ice-cold room, which consisted of hot coffee and tea, toast, and boiled eggs. We forced ourselves to take in as much food as possible.

We knew we would have a long day and probably not much chance to eat further, but nobody was particularly hungry. For us it was due more to the early morning hour, than altitude. Luckily, the altitude affected the three of us very little, while some of the others, especially Uschi and Shell, were still complaining of headaches and simply couldn't eat.

It took determination to dress in full mountain gear in the middle of the night when it was freezing cold. There was some comfort in having a group of people around performing the same tasks, with the same motivation, but few words were spoken. The light in the room was meager, but sufficient for the task.

At this altitude, it took over an hour just to get dressed. It was important to dress in layers, to provide the opportunity to adjust the body temperature. If you dress too warm, you lose valuable water due to increased perspiration, too cold and you use extra energy trying to keep warm.

I had underwear, thermal underwear, and my regular hiking pants to cover my legs. For my torso, I wore a thin undershirt, a long sleeved hiking shirt, a pullover, and a Gortex parka. I pulled a wool cap on to keep my head and ears warm, and my jacket had a hood to keep the wind off my neck and head.

I jammed my feet into thin polypropylene liners, thick woolen socks, and my mid-weight hiking boots. We had decided on mid-weight hiking boots because we were not wearing crampons and should not encounter too much snow and ice.

We secured gaiters with steel hooks over the boots and the lower part of the pants. Gaiters are tight fitting leggings made of strong fabric that attach to the upper part of the boots and hug the calf portion of the leg below the knee. They are worn in snow and ice, or loose sand and gravel, to prevent material from entering the shoes and socks.

I strapped on a small "fanny pack" that contained a small flashlight, a battery-operated 35-millimeter camera, some snacks, and a half-liter bottle of water. In addition, I shouldered a full day pack with emergency items like a first aid kit, extra shoe laces, extra gloves, some rope, sun screen, etc., a manually operated 35-millimeter camera (in case it was so cold the battery-operated camera refused to work), glacier glasses, three liters of water, and some additional food.

When we wanted to remove layers of clothing, it would be convenient to stuff them in the pack. Lastly, I wore thin glove liners inside my thick gloves to keep my hands and fingers warm. Diane and Kyle dressed similarly, paying close attention to layering.

Diane had difficulties with her gaiters, so I knelt down on the cold stone floor and secured them tightly to her boots and legs. She crammed glacier glasses, two water bottles, half a liter each, and a couple of candy bars into a small fanny pack. During the final stages of dressing one of the clasps on her fanny pack broke. Fred and I fumbled with it, made a good field repair, and we were ready to go.

Uschi, Gerd, Michelle, and their guides had already left. We finally stepped out of the stone walled hut into the arctic chill and were greeted by a crystal clear sky filled with brilliant stars. A nearly full moon hovered over neighboring Mawenzi, drenching the pumice below our boots in a spectral glow, casting unsettling shadows.

We packed flashlights and headlamps, but the bright moonlight rendered them unnecessary. The temperature was brutally cold, well below freezing, but there was virtually no wind. Since we were dressed for the conditions, it seemed perfect for a summit attempt.

Briskly, we dashed onto the rocky trail leading almost straight up the towering volcano. In the moonlight, the scree field had a surreal, shiny gray appearance that extended up into the black sky beyond our field of vision. It seemed to go on forever.

We were about the fourth group of climbers to finally leave the Kibo hut that morning. It was after 1:30 A.M. by the time we hit the trail.

Fred led our group initially. I was directly behind him, followed by Kyle, and Diane brought up the rear. Fred knew the trail and being the good guide he is, he adjusted the pace according to our needs. When we crowded him, he sped up slightly. If a gap opened up between us, he slowed a tad. He frequently looked back to check on Diane and Kyle and made sure the group was doing well.

We traveled as a fairly tight foursome. Fred chose a path that skirted the main scree field, where the gravel was loosest. That way the footing was reasonably good. In a short time we came up to another group and passed them on the wide trail.

We plodded up the steep volcanic slope with a steady pace. A while later, we passed a second group of climbers, and a short time later another. The last group we passed were Gary, Shell, and Randy, which surprised me, because they were about our age or younger and looked to be in good shape.

They had started almost a half an hour before us and it only took us an hour to catch them. As we scampered by them, I said, "Looks like you're on the slow escalator." "You go ahead," they muttered. "We'll pass you when you're puking your guts out higher on the mountain." "Fat chance." But the thin air and our swift pace did contribute to an exhausting climb up the steepest part of the mountain.

CRUNCH, CRUNCH, CRUNCH was the only sound as

we plodded up the trail. We were making good progress and time had no meaning at all. We were mesmerized by the activity at hand. One step in front of the other.

Kyle sang songs to himself and anything else he knew by heart to pass the slow time up the slope. I had no idea how much time had gone by or how we were doing, although we felt good, and we were passing other climbers who were mostly young men. We stepped onto a nearly level plateau where there was a small overhang.

On close inspection, it turned out to be a small cave, the same cave Hans Meyer had discovered during his successful summit bid over one hundred years ago. We had seen this feature the day before when we were inspecting the trail from below. It was nearly halfway up the scree field.

We paused for a small drink of water. I decided to take a few bites of a chocolate bar. It was difficult to chew, but I forced it down to maintain my energy. At this altitude, the smallest action takes a great deal of effort and that includes eating. In addition, nothing seems to taste good, probably because the taste buds go on strike at high altitude.

Diane had stuffed some candy bars in her jacket and ate them along the way. For her it required planning because she was using two hiking poles, making it nerve-racking just to eat and ascend the tricky terrain.

Above the cave, Kyle and I had some conversation, which Diane overheard. We were discussing how many steps it would take to get from the Kibo hut to Uhuru Peak.

Probably because we had nothing better to do, we were actually going through the math: "... Okay in round numbers, the hut is at 4700 meters and the peak at 5900 meters for an elevation difference of about 1200 meters ... blah, blah, blah ... Assuming the average incline is about thirty percent . . . blah, blah, blah . . . with switchbacks that results in a total distance traveled of something greater than 3000 meters. If each step is about . . . blah, blah, blah. . . it will take over ten thousand steps, one way. . . "

Ten thousand steps! Diane couldn't believe her ears, because that made it sound so far and tedious. It made her wish she had not heard the numbers. She went back to concentrating on ascending the scree field, which seemed to go on for a long time. Then she got into a groove — almost like a trance or hypnotic state.

The trail steepened to approximately forty degrees. We continued up the trail and followed the meandering route set by Fred. The serpentines were firm and the climb up not too difficult. But then the path crossed the loose scree field and the footing turned sour. All of a sudden, it was like walking in a large bowl of mashed potatoes. Our boots dug into the scree at almost the same rate as our forward progress.

At this altitude, it was a difficult way to proceed. Even with the sliding and occasionally stumbling I felt in control and was not worried about my balance. When we traversed the scree, it became better again. Another serpentine and the routine with the mashed potatoes started over again. Kyle was getting pretty good traction and felt secure in his progress. Diane struggled a bit, but negotiated these risky stretches by effective use of her poles.

My boots sank so deeply into the scree that it looked like I was slipping and sliding on the steep incline. When Kyle asked if I was all right after such a slip, I told him I was fine and that it was part of my method of ascending the tricky scree. I called it "controlled stumbling."

I later explained that I purposely kept my body leaning into the mountain, so when I did slide, my weight would shift forward, toward the scree, instead of away from the gravel and down the slope. Kyle and Diane would make fun of me later on, because they thought I looked like a drunken sailor when I used this "controlled stumbling."

We were pressure breathing, a technique used to force air to stay in the lungs longer to maximize absorption of oxygen by the body. Occasionally, we stopped to take five or six deep breaths before continuing. The air was thin.

At this altitude, there is less than half as much oxygen than at sea level, only forty-eight percent to be precise. We could all feel it, but we were still making good progress up the mountain. If a person were dropped here from sea level by a helicopter, he or she would pass out within a few minutes, because of the thin air and lack of acclimatization.

Occasionally, I turned around to see how Diane and Kyle were doing. They were both right there moving up strongly. I was so glad to see them making such good progress, in spite of our limited acclimatization. Especially Diane, because she had the most fear to overcome. However, she dug down deep and found the muscle and mental toughness to keep going.

I looked up and saw an eerie slope of mountain still ahead of us before the black, jagged horizon blended in with the black night sky. We continued plodding up the trail, traversing the scree field numerous times, each time repeating the mashed potato routine. We resembled animals fighting quicksand. Then we entered a labyrinth of massive boulders, some the size of small trucks, interspersed along the scree and the trail got even steeper. We had to make our way gingerly through the boulders.

Some were unstable and occasionally shot down the mountain with the force of a herd of buffaloes. The story of the Norwegian climber blasting down the slope was very much on my mind every time I had to grip a rock. More than once, I had the distinct feeling that the boulders were moving. It was difficult to judge if there was real movement or if it was in all in my mind.

I was concerned for myself and all the climbers below me, especially Diane and Kyle. Between the rocks were patches of layered ice that crunched below our feet, creating some very slippery terrain and we were forced to use the solid boulders to keep from slipping.

The last two hundred vertical meters before reaching the crater rim were definitely the hardest part for Kyle. It was the most difficult terrain on the mountain, and since we were not wearing crampons, it got slippery and treacherous at times. This high in the atmosphere there were strong gusts of icy cold wind that we fought, while weaving our way through the rocks and ice.

Almost everything we stepped on — the scree, the ice, the rocks — would slide out from under us. Because of the steep grade, Kyle really had to lift his legs up high to make progress and find stable footing. It was difficult to find ground that wouldn't give way when weight was applied. But we were closing in on the crater rim.

Diane liked this part of the trail, because it was distinctly different from the previous section of trail, and she knew we were closer to the crater rim. We continued to lumber higher and higher, up and over, and through the rocks. The moon was shining so brightly that the shadows from the rocks obscured the trail, so we were forced to stumble along blindly on the unknown ground. By this time I was leading, with Kyle right behind. Fred was closest to Diane warning her to be careful.

A moment later I noticed the star-studded sky met the mountain upwards from my vantage point, but amazingly not too far away. We continued clambering between the rocks, over the scree and up the mountain. It was hard to believe, but we must have been at this for hours, because suddenly, as I wrestled up the last steps, I was on the crater rim.

The surroundings changed dramatically. Instead of a dark field in front of me, there were thousands of stars suspended in the frozen sky above large snow-covered fields. The bright moonlight bathed the scenery, giving it an intriguing fluorescent glow.

Moments later my son followed and turned around to enjoy the three-hundred-sixty degree view. Mawenzi was visible in the bright moonlight and looked diminutive from our elevated aerie. He saw Diane and Fred just below him and urged, "Mom, just a few more steps and you'll be on the crater rim."

Kyle was exhausted, but once on the crater rim he felt better and more energetic. Maybe it was because he could see where the peak was and he knew the hardest part was behind him. He said it was just like when he and I had climbed Mount Whitney in 1993 when he was thirteen.

Near the top of Whitney, the trail meanders up a long steep incline, commonly known as "Ninety Nine Switchbacks." This section is grueling due to the altitude and the rough terrain. He had a lot of trouble struggling up the last part of the switchbacks, and I can remember coaxing him, "Kyle you're doing fantastic. This is the hardest part of the climb and you're almost done with it. Just a few more steps. Then rest a moment, and we'll knock this baby off together."

With those encouraging words and his strong will, he made it. When he finally reached the top of the switchbacks, called Discovery Pinnacle, we got a fabulous view of the Sierra Nevada mountain range to the east and west. Then he quickly got his second wind and from that point on he cruised to the summit feeling great. Later he told me that was exactly how he felt as he climbed along the crater rim of Kilimanjaro.

We took a few steps along the ridge, which made a distinct bend, and there was Gillman's Point. Kyle thought, "I wonder what the sunrise will look like from the peak?" With that thought in mind, he continued up the dark trail along the crater rim.

Diane was relieved, not only to be on level ground, but her ankle was holding up and didn't bother her, at least so far. She was still worried about the descent, especially down the steep scree field.

Stepping onto the level crater rim briefly gave Diane the illusion that the climb was over. She almost felt like we were "on top." Emotionally there was a sigh of relief, but intellectually she knew better and there was one more major hurdle ahead of us. Fred pointed out, "Here Gillman's."

She had expected a summit-like top, but there were no exceptional physical features; it was just a small outcrop with a sign on one end. It was brutally cold and the sky seemed more brilliant to her. Maybe it was her imagination or the reflection of the moonlight on the snow. On the other hand, maybe everything just looked dazzling, because the hardest part of the climb was over.

I continued hiking past Gillman's just as if it were not a landmark, as the conversation we had in Johannesburg flashed into my mind. I was feeling strong and there was no way that I was going to wimp out at Gillman's.

Unknowingly I had distanced myself from the group. Fred called over and I waited by a shear rock wall, which gave me a good opportunity to take a leak. After everyone caught up with me, we hiked for awhile along the crater rim with only a gentle incline.

So far, the experience had been monumental, especially being with my family. At one point on the trail Diane said to us, "There's no place I'd rather be right now than with the two of you right here." And I believe that's what mattered most to her, not reaching the summit at all cost, but the camaraderie and the closeness she felt to her two men. A paragraph from the book *Doctor Zhivago* came to mind. It reads in part:

> *"And so it turned out that only life similar to the life of those around us,*
> *merging with it without a ripple, is genuine life, and that an unshared*
> *happiness is not happiness . . . And this was most vexing of all."*

At this moment it rang so true that real happiness is shared happiness, and we all felt it, working hard in the bitter cold on the crater plateau.

Even though we had been climbing for many hours, the star-studded sky was still black with no hint of daylight. When we started this odyssey we had only a vague idea how big this mountain was. But, I was enjoying myself and felt myself getting stronger as I got higher. I also knew that Diane and Kyle had not trained as much as they would have liked and there was the possibility that they could run out of steam as we got higher. I just hoped that when this was all over we would all think it was worth it.

I started wondering just where the summit was, and if we would ever get there. Then the grade increased to perhaps fifteen to twenty percent and climbing became more difficult. The subzero temperatures, the fierce wind, and the lack of oxygen all conspired to produce a hostile environment. Our lungs were pumping like two-stroke engines trying to suck in enough air. I had to stop, hunker down, and take several deep breaths before continuing.

As we continued along the crater rim, we skirted several tall glacier walls. We could hear creaking and groaning noises emanating from the grotesque ice formations. It was a strange and mythical setting. The entire landscape was enigmatic. We were on the equator, yet towering ice walls surrounded us and we faced a freezing wind more reminiscent of Alaska in winter than Africa in summer.

This part of the crater rim was frightfully exposed. The savage wind ripped across the rocky terrain and was filled with flaying specks of dust and sand that stung our faces. The ferocious wind chill pummeled us as we worked our way up the trail. It was brutally cold, perhaps as much as twenty or thirty degrees below zero. The sign at the trailhead was correct when it said that the climate at the peak was Arctic.

We came upon a field of large patches of ice that protruded from the ground resembling giant inverted shark's teeth. They were sharp, wind-swept pinnacles of ice that were all around us, about waist high, glowing a ghostly white in the moonlight. These swords of ice splintered under our heavy steps. It was beautiful and fascinating, but we just kept ascending. Apparently, Kyle got a case of summit fever, because he suddenly picked up his pace and pulled ahead of us.

Trudging slowly up the rocky trail in the predawn light, I glanced ahead and could barely make out the summit marker. I slowed so Diane could catch up to me, and as she approached she thought the ice-cold wind and the thin air were playing tricks on her mind.

Could this really be the summit, and not just another false crest? In an almost magical moment, we strolled up the last few steps arm-in-arm to the summit together. Kyle was already there waiting for us and we were all fired up when we joined him.

We'd arrived on Uhuru Peak, the white roof of Africa, one of the seven summits, and we did it as a family! We hugged, embraced each other, laughed and cried, all at the same time. We couldn't believe it; we were finally on top. It seemed like all the effort to get to this point had bottled up a huge fountain of emotional energy.

This had been the best summit day we had ever experienced. Once Diane focused her eyes she saw the large, wooden sign and read it out loud: "YOU ARE NOW AT THE UHURU PEAK, THE HIGHEST POINT IN AFRICA. ALTITUDE 5895 METERS ABOVE SEA LEVEL." She just stared at it in amazement, Uhuru Peak — 5895 meters, a personal altitude record for us.

Approaching the top, Kyle started wearing out again. The last stretch up to the summit was a gentle incline, but the wind's cold blade stabbed continuously at his back and pierced his heavy thermal insulation. Even with thick gloves, his hands were freezing and he told me later, "It felt like they had turned to ice." He desperately needed some body heat, so he sped up, to try to generate some internal combustion. It worked for a short time, but then he crested a small hump in the trail and focused on some boxes.

At first, it didn't even seem strange to him that there was a pile of boxes and poles. The lack of oxygen kept him from thinking clearly. When he reached the boxes, there was no where else to go, and it finally occurred to him, "I'm on the summit!" The faint light of the moon had cloaked the summit until he was right on top of it. It felt great to finally reach our goal and for a short time, he forgot about his cold hands.

Success at dawn! Here we are on the summit of Kilimanjaro, the highest peak in Africa.

I felt proud of both Kyle and Diane, but for different reasons. For Kyle, because as a teenager he really did not share much of his life with us anymore. To have him with us on this climb was a tremendous privilege. We learned so much about him in the previous few days.

Although he complained about the bitter cold and the hard work, he realized it was a fantastic experience, especially at this young age. I had not been too concerned about his ability to climb the mountain for two reasons.

One, he had performed well on all the previous climbs. Even without proper training, I knew he was tough. And two, he was endowed with the exuberance of youth. He didn't worry about all the things that might go wrong or even think that anything could go wrong. The attitude of the young is — just do it!

With Diane, it was different. When we flew over the mountain a few days before, she became quiet and introverted, which is unusual for her, and I knew why. The mountain had scared her. She didn't know if she would be able to make it.

She was unable to train vigorously for this climb due to her tendon and ankle problems. However, even with those deep fears she attempted the climb, determined to go as far as possible. And not only did she go all the way to the summit, she went strongly.

She was right there with us. She overcame her deep fears and powered up the mountain, gaining confidence with each step, with each switchback up the scree field. On Uhuru Peak, we all felt a powerful family bond of having accomplished a world-class feat together.

I was so proud to be standing there with the two people I loved most in this world. Tears blurred my eyes. I think one of the last times I cried was in the delivery room when Kyle was born. This was a very powerful moment for me.

Over the years, we have climbed a lot of mountains. Diane and I climbed most of them together. Kyle joined us on many mountains, mostly in his early teenage years. Just by circumstance, most of the more interesting climbs he did with me.

We scaled San Jacinto in the middle of winter in deep snow while Diane was recovering from inflamed Psoais and Iliacus tendons in her hip. When we went to Mount Whitney, she was nursing a sore Iliacus tendon. Climbing the Breithorn, a storm was brewing and she stayed with the in-laws.

On top of Kili, it really hit her how special it was to be with her two guys on a major summit, and to have spent the time and effort to get there together. Certainly, parents of teenagers can relate to how little quality time is spent with them. The teenage problems had melted away, at least during this trip.

Nevertheless, there was also a long-term effect. This experience significantly altered Kyle's attitude toward us and life in general, and we noticed it long after we had returned home. It was not like he "grew up" during this short trip, but he did take a small leap in his maturity.

We reached the summit a little before 6:00 A.M., so it took us a little over four hours from Kibo hut. The sign at the trailhead said five hours to Gillman's Point plus another one and a half hours to Uhuru Peak for a total of six and a half hours. Obviously, we had made it in good time.

It was still pitch black, but the faint suggestion of dawn was already coloring the rim of the northeastern sky with a fiery yellow-orange band. With a slower ascent, we would have been bathed in sunlight as we scampered up to the summit plateau. However, our pace gave us the opportunity to experience a sunrise from the top of the African continent.

The climb to the summit was less exhausting than I anticipated. Perhaps all the time on the stair master and the Leg Blaster, running up and down the neighborhood hills, and climbing the local mountains was more than needed.

Maybe, in a sense, I had trained too much. But the physical conditioning allowed me to maintain an inner peace, and not get rattled or intimidated by the mountain. This mind set, and the physical and mental conditioning, gave me a serene assurance that I could scale Kilimanjaro. Indeed, I never doubted my ability to summit.

Not that I was overconfident, because I know lots of things can happen: inclement weather, food and water can disagree with you, altitude-related problems can hit you, especially when there is only limited time to acclimatize, a sprained ankle or a pulled muscle, the list goes on and on.

Kilimanjaro Adventure

Once you achieve this mental state, you gain an inner feeling of calm and confidence. I don't want to get too mystical, but this state of confidence is half the success of mountain climbing. Reaching the summit is merely a consequence of this state.

We had to capture our accomplishment on film as a record of this fine moment. We snapped a few pictures of each other on the summit. A black box containing the summit register, and a few poles stuck in the ground, marked the summit. Nearby was the sign that used to be part of the summit marker. I had seen pictures of it. It was just lying on the ground. I picked up the sign, placed it on the box, and propped it up against the poles in front of us. It looked like it belonged there.

We handed the camera to another climber who had arrived at the summit via another route shortly after us. He took one picture and tried to return the camera to me. I asked him to take another one. And another one. It was a good thing I had asked him to take three pictures. Only one of them turned out. The other two had our heads cut off and had our feet nicely centered. Well, he was a mountain climber, not a photographer.

By now, the sun slowly peeked over the jagged eastern horizon. This close to the equator the sunrises and sunsets are abrupt. We encouraged Fred to get in one of the pictures. He needed a moment to get ready.

Apparently, the air was not thin enough for his acclimatized lungs. He had to light up a cigarette and filter the fresh mountain air through the burning cigarette to get the full effect of the altitude. After he smoked the cigarette, he was ready for the picture. We read some of the comments in the ledger and then added our own words of joy.

Standing on Uhuru Peak, Kyle felt a surge of adrenaline and a sense of power, as if he could accomplish anything. He remembered then that at one of the lower camps, one of the doctors was sizing him up while they were talking. He had questioned Kyle's ability to reach the summit. It was especially satisfying for Kyle to make the summit because of that comment. We later found out that that doctor didn't even make Gillman's Point. That poor guy will never know what it feels like to reach the summit.

The sunrise at the summit was one of the most spectacular sights I've ever seen in nature. The fiery yellow and orange colors burst onto the dark sky with such magical speed that it seemed like the beginning of the world, and not just the beginning of another day.

The black sky turned pristine sky blue in a matter of a few fleeting moments. The incredible mixing of night and day and the quick changes of color created a biblical image of what the first day of creation might have been like, when God created the earth and the sun, and divided light from darkness.

The crater landscape took on an entirely new perspective in the sunlight that had remained hidden from us during the ascent in the dark. We could see more detail and greater distances. Fresh snow covered most of the gently rolling slopes that make up the large crater plateau.

There are three large glacier fields surrounding the central crater and all three became visible, glowing an iridescent blue caused by the scattering of sunlight from deep within the crystalline ice. A multitude of lesser peaks pierced the cloud cover below us to reveal their presence.

We loitered on the roof of Africa for about a half an hour before I said, "Let's head back down before we freeze our butts off." I reached down, grabbed a few small volcanic rocks from the rugged terrain, and tucked the souvenirs in my jacket pocket for closer inspection and reflection of this monumental moment later on. By now, the sunlight glinted off the fresh snow blanketing the wind-scoured expanse of the crater plateau.

A few minutes into the descent, we met our bunkmates from the Kibo hut, Gary, Shell, and Randy. They looked a little ashen and moved slowly, but they were making good progress up the final slope. "Hey, it's about time you guys dragged your carcasses up here. There's a group waiting for you at the summit," I remarked.

"You're an animal. I can't believe you got so far ahead of us," Gary replied. "What's your secret?" "No secret, we just kept going till we couldn't go any higher. Congratulations, you'll love it up there." And then we high-fived them before we proceeded down along the crater rim.

Edge of southern icefield with jagged firn in foreground. Tanzania is shrouded in cloud cover.

Half an hour later we came across an extremely exhausted woman. She looked pale as a ghost. It took a moment to register, but it was Michelle. She was obviously suffering from acute mountain sickness. "How are you feeling?" I asked. "Not so good. I've vomited a couple of times and I'm really tired and dizzy. I don't know if I'll be able to make it much further."

"That's okay, because you don't have much further to go. The summit is right over that small crest there," I replied, trying to sound encouraging, as I pointed up the trail.

She was resting on a large rock next to her guide. When Fred saw the two, he immediately told her to stand up and continue. There is a great danger at high altitude to get too comfortable resting. The mind and the body can fall into a state of relaxation and refuse to go further. In a guided situation, the problem is not want-

Sun and wind carved ice pinnacles along crater rim with Diane, Kyle, and Fred.

ing to continue to fight and reach the summit; but unguided it is easy to rest to the point of falling asleep and remaining in place so long that you freeze to death.

The assistant guide, in his inexperience, didn't consider that. Or perhaps he didn't want to push to the summit himself if the client didn't demand it. After Fred rousted her, she moved toward the summit at a snails pace, but given how close she was, she was going to make it.

Because it was getting light quickly now, we were able to enjoy the stunning views in sunlight. We snapped some pictures of the landscape on top of Kibo. The crater region is a large, relatively flat expanse but not very deep. It was not well defined from our vantage point. Because of our location, we couldn't see into the Reusch crater, just the mound leading up to it.

View of Reusch crater. Eastern icefield cascades along the crater rim in background.

The sky was clear and we could see forever. We were overlooking all of Africa. However, we were above the clouds and we saw little detail because of the great altitude. Thick cloud cover below us obscured the plains of Kenya and Tanzania. We could make out Mount Meru toward the west and a few other smaller volcanoes poking through the clouds.

We were hoping to get a glimpse of Mount Kenya toward the north. It's about 300 kilometers away and supposedly can be seen on an extremely clear day. That is one of the greatest distances that can be seen between two distinct locations on the surface of the planet. However, we were not lucky enough to see it that day.

We descended to Gillman's Point, snapped a couple of photos and headed down the steep cone. Once we maneuvered past the ice and boulders, the long scree field opened up. Kyle looked at it with delight and without hesitation raced down, letting gravity do all the work.

The surface was ideally suited to take big lunges and then have the soft gravel absorb the shock in time to get ready for the next lunge, a technique known as plunge stepping. Using this technique, Kyle flew down the field in no time.

Reaching the summit was only the halfway mark of the climb, but at least the rest was all downhill. The downhill part requires less work, because gravity is in your favor, but it is harder on the body, especially the joints.

Diane was becoming fully aware of the biomechanics of mountain climbing. She was exhausted and she was struggling. We stayed close together as we worked our way down the scree field, one small step at a time. The descent was torturous on her poor knees.

Half way down the scree field the bones in her knees felt

Kyle racing down the scree field. Fred is on left.

like they were grinding the nerves to a pulp. With every step, she received a sharp blow of pain. By now, she was using her hiking poles like crutches for some gratifying relief. Fred reminded her: "Take it slow and easy, it be better for your ankle and knees."

All of us were exhausted, because we had been awake for hours with only some meager snacks to eat all day. We continued to make our way slowly down the scree field toward Kibo hut. The sun was starting to warm our feeble bones, especially with our thick clothes.

We peeled off layers of clothing to make the temperature more bearable. Then we caught a glimpse of the Kibo hut downhill from us, and Diane started envisioning the comfort of reaching the soothing bunks.

About an hour later as we approached the Kibo hut, we saw one of the young porters carrying something as he walked toward us. In broken English he said, "Hot tea and biscuits for you." This was exactly what we needed. We were worn out and ready for a snack and a little rest.

Kyle was cocooned in his sleeping bag. In addition to the tea and biscuits, we had some orange slices, which tasted great. They were juicy and provided some necessary carbohydrates. We rested for a short time flat on our backs and then packed our gear for the hike back down.

We had to chase Kyle out of the bunk and then we started the hike back to the Horombo camp. Uschi and Gerd, who had turned around at Gillman's Point, had left Kibo hut at least a half an hour before Diane and I arrived. However, they had seen Kyle, and he filled them in on our successful summit bid.

As we descended the trail, we bumped into many climbers

Diane near bottom of scree field. The hardest part is definitely behind us.

we had met previously at the lower camps. Before we could even open our mouths, they would say, "Congratulations, we heard from Uschi and Gerd that all three of you made the summit. How was it?" Sometimes, news travels fast on the mountain. We ran into numerous groups of people, with whom we chatted and relayed our experience.

The group of doctors was particularly interested in our ordeal and we had a lengthy conversation with them. They asked things like, "Did the thin air bother you? How much water did you drink? Did you take Diamox? A full tablet in the morning or half a tablet in the morning and half in the evening?" Allen was quieter than normal. Perhaps he had predicted that we were going to have trouble reaching the summit and was eating his words.

Nevertheless, everyone was happy for us. We were known as "the family" in everyone's conversation and then we became "the family that summited Uhuru Peak." We came upon our graduate student friends, Ellef and Micke, as they were struggling their way toward the Kibo hut.

Ellef looked reasonably strong, but Micke looked as weak as a newborn gazelle on the African plains. Diane told them, "If we can make it, so can you, you're almost twenty years younger than we are. Good luck on your final assault." Although we were thinking Ellef might make it, we wondered about Micke's chances to summit.

We continued the descent for another three hours, when we finally dragged our tired bodies into the Horombo camp. We were beat by now. As Kyle put it, "We'd hiked for too long and were clinically dead when we stumbled into camp." Fred had arranged for huts and our bags were safely stored inside. We pulled out our sleeping bags and took a well-deserved nap.

Before dinner, I chatted with Michelle and asked, "Did

you find your camera?" "No, I went back and looked everywhere. I asked around the camp, but nobody had seen it," she replied. "I didn't use my back-up camera on the summit, so here, you take it for the rest of your trip," I said. She thanked me and stashed it in her backpack.

Getting to the top of Kilimanjaro was going through Kyle's mind and that was when the achievement really hit him. Conquering the summit of Kilimanjaro had been the hardest thing he had done in his young life. He thought about how hard it was and how everything else he did from now on would be fairly easy compared to that. It's only partially true, but his teenage mind was on the right track.

He told me that he was sore everywhere, especially his legs and lower back. It would take days before he could take a step without feeling the lactic acid that had built up in his muscles. When he saw me walking without being sore or stiff, he realized that he should have trained more. He correctly thought that if he had trained and exercised his legs more, he probably would have felt stronger on the final ascent and would not have been so sore afterwards.

The porters finally served dinner, but our appetite was low. We had eaten very little and had had a very strenuous day. Our stomachs should have been completely empty, but our systems were still geared up. Although the food was generally good, it was starting to taste all the same.

During dinner, we discussed the day with our climbing group. Of the six people in our group, four had summited Uhuru Peak. Uschi and Gerd were proud that they had reached Gillman's Point. It was a true accomplishment for them.

They were in their late fifties and while they hiked a little in their local Alps, they were not serious mountain climbers. Michelle had a struggle and not the best guide, but was able to summit. Our family did extremely well. We made the top in good time; still I felt that I could have gone higher, and I believe the same is true for Diane and Kyle. How much higher? We'll have to explore that on another mountain.

So everyone felt good about their accomplishments and, most important, nobody got hurt. The only casualty was a large rip in the seat of my Khaki pants, probably because of a brush with one of the boulders on the top part of the scree field.

We all slept well that night, and after breakfast we started the long descent down to the Mandara encampment for a short lunch break and then down to the park entrance. The weather for

Still able to stand at Horombo after our successful summit bid. Left to right: Gerd, Uschi, Fred, Kyle, Diane, Michelle, and Hal.

the descent was superb. While we were in the moorlands, the sun frequently moved behind clouds, and the intense UV's did not scorch us. But we still had nice views of the big open plains and plant-covered, rolling hills.

On the way down, I asked Diane, "What did you think of the trail we took?" Without hesitation she replied, "It was fantastic. I liked the Marangu trail, even though it is the tourist route and supposedly the least scenic. I think that's nonsense. We had a wonderful time and I don't regret for one moment taking this route. The huts were comfortable, which made the camping experience less primitive. It was fun meeting all the other people and making new friends. The conditions at the camps didn't detract from the mountain and, if anything, made it more memorable. Our experience was better than we could've hoped for. It never entered my mind that we had settled on an inferior route."

I thought the same, but still would have preferred taking the Machame route up, and the Marangu route down climbing over the mountain. I enjoyed every aspect of the mountain and the people we met. The last push to the summit separated the men from the boys. Only the tough climbers reached the summit and the tourist climbers were left behind.

Clearly, if you want solitude and do not want to share the mountain with other climbers, you need to take one of the less traveled routes. On some of them, you are guaranteed not to encounter another soul. However, the scenery on the Marangu trail is spectacular. Other routes also have spectacular scenery, but it is just different, not better.

When Diane had time to reflect on the whole experience, she felt charged up by it. She told me it really boosted her self-confidence to have accomplished something as physically demanding as summiting Kilimanjaro. It made her feel stronger than before. Later, for example, work-related problems paled by comparison to the effort exerted on the mountain.

We descended the forested trail to the park entrance. We ran back into the small gift shop where we bought a few items, including some overpriced postcards, to inform our friends and family that we had a successful climb. The money goes to maintain the park, so we did not feel ripped off, but rather viewed it as supporting something we enjoyed.

Then it was time to "tip" the guides and porters. The Tanzanian Park service pays the guides and porters, but they make pitiful wages. They rely on the generosity of the climbers for their real income. We had discussed the tip earlier in the day and our group had elected me to handle this part of the trek.

Fred and I spoke, and he agreed with everything that we had decided. His only comment was that the porters worked hard and he hoped that we took that into consideration. The profoundly generous quality of our group made the situation easy.

The only sensitive point was that one of the two assistant guides had asked for money from Uschi and Gerd on the morning of the summit day, which they had given to him. We subtracted that amount from the total tip, explaining it to Fred. He seemed to understand, but I'm certain that he would have a few words with that particular assistant guide about compromising the client/guide relationship by asking for money just before the summit attempt.

Not once on the entire trek had Fred brought up the subject of money, which spoke highly of his character. In addition to the monetary tip, I pulled out a clean T-shirt, probably the last clean one I still had, a good sweatshirt, and an extra pair of hiking boots and handed them all to Fred.

His eyes lit up with joy when he clutched the shirts, and especially the boots. In addition, we had a cache of goodies in one of our bags. We pulled out a load of cookies and chocolates and gave it to Fred. He was the head guide and would take care of his people as he saw fit.

Weeks later, we heard from our graduate student friends, Ellef and Micke. They filled us in on their summit attempt. In Ellef's own words:

> "...I can tell you that I started to experience high-altitude sickness above Kibo hut, despite heavy intake of water and extreme pole walking. On the way up to Gillman's Point I got extremely tired and lost some presence of mind (hypoxia). I could only take ten steps at a time before I had to sit down and rest.
> When I finally reached Gillman's Point at sunrise, as the last member of my group, I was almost delirious and started to cry. I managed to have Micke take one photo of me and my guide in front of the sign at Gillman's Point. I was too tired to even handle a camera and take a picture. I turned toward Uhuru Peak, but reaching Gillman's and the rim of the crater gave me the impression that I had climbed Kilimanjaro, so I gave up. A decision I almost regret now, but that is easy to say at 10 meters above sea level.
> Anyway, Micke almost recovered from his illness and made it to the summit, as did the serious Spanish gentlemen, the Dutch couple, and the German group."

The altitude hit Ellef hard, and Micke made the summit. I

Kilimanjaro Adventure

never would have guessed that, and would have bet money that it would have been the other way around. It just shows that first impressions can be deceptive.

As for the group of South African doctors, the information we received was somewhat sketchy and we didn't get all the details. However, this is what we found out. Apparently none of them reached Uhuru Peak. Two of them made it to Gillman's Point. We suspect Allen accompanied one semi-ambitious doctor up the tortuous scree field to the crater rim. None of the others got close, although they all made it to the Kibo hut.

Worst of all, one of the women in the group became violently ill and had to be transported down the mountain to the hospital. Small rescue carts are stored at all the encampments just for such emergencies. There is a large hospital, the Kilimanjaro Christian Medical Center in Moshi, to deal with emergency cases.

She was fortunate to have been with a group of medical doctors who were on the mountain to experience first hand some of the effects of altitude. We heard she recovered quickly. Mountains are beautiful and it is enjoyable to climb them, but you have to be prepared for them and have respect for them.

In the early part of the century, Dr. Reusch became intensely involved in the exploration of Kilimanjaro and reached the summit on several occasions. In recognition of his accomplishments, he was appointed the Honorary President of the Mountain Club of East Africa. In that position, he instituted the ritual of presenting a braided wreath intertwined with dried flowers to every person who reaches the summit.

That tradition has been maintained to the present, except that the wreath has been replaced with a certificate. The Tanzanian Ministry of Tourism and Information awarded such a certificate to Dr. Hans Meyer posthumously on the 80th anniversary of his first ascent.

Today's certificate has the emblem of the Tanzania National Park, a sketch of Kilimanjaro and states that the person has successfully climbed Mount Kilimanjaro, the highest peak in Africa, right to the summit - Uhuru Peak - 5895 meters. It states the person's name and age, and the date and time of the summit ascent.

The guide and the Kilimanjaro National Park Warden sign it, and it has a stamped signature of the Director General of the Tanzania National Parks. Every certificate is numbered. Ours are numbers 6309/97, 6311/97, and 6360/97. There is also a certificate for reaching Gillman's Point, which looks similar, except for the wording and it has a green border instead of a gold border. This is a very nice memento from the Tanzania National Parks administration.

James was waiting by the van for the drive down the hill to Moshi. We bid a warm "Kwa Heri" to Fred and our porters, and headed back to Moshi where we said "Auf Wiedersehn" to Uschi and Gerd and returned to the Springland with Michelle.

We got the same room as before the climb. We piled our gear in the room and Diane bolted for the bathroom. Thank God, there was hot water, which is not always the case in Moshi, because of problems with the power distribution system.

We all washed thoroughly. There is nothing like getting cleaned up after spending several days getting dirty on a mountain. We lay around on the beds, relaxed, and talked about our impressions of the climb.

Dinner was served outside in the courtyard and consisted of sweet and sour pork and chow mein as the main course. None of us had a strong appetite yet, but at least the food tasted better

Kilimanjaro Adventure

than on the mountain. The next day we said "Good Bye" to Michelle and headed into Moshi.

Moshi is situated on a flat dusty plain with no apparent city planning. The 20,000 or so inhabitants live in shacks and structures that are strewn randomly along the sides of the existing paved and unpaved roads. The commercial downtown district is filled with hotels, offices, and shops. The central open-air market is choked with one-man sale stands and street hustlers.

It is nothing like a town the same size in the United States, but more like something you'd see in an *Indiana Jones* movie. Our driver warned us that it's not safe for tourists, but it seemed too interesting to avoid. We got caught up in the simple joy of walking in an exotic country and, ignoring James's advice did a little exploring in the bustling market before our bus arrived.

We bought some oranges and bananas and ate them on the spot. We also bought a few gifts and things for our friends and relatives back home. Some of the "buying" turned into "trading," where the merchants wanted our glacier glasses, or Kyle's walkman, or some of the other items on us, in exchange for their wares. In addition, they always asked for ballpoint pens; apparently there is a general shortage of pens in East Africa.

This part of going to the mountains is fun, because you get to experience different people and cultures and see how they live and do things. When our bus finally showed up, we piled in and headed back to Nairobi for the second part of our African adventure, a photo safari to the Masai Mara National Game Park.

8

Safari

Lounging comfortably in the air-conditioned bus back to Nairobi, we could hear the faint whirl of the tires on the rough pavement. The soothing sights and sounds allowed our minds to wander and relive the experience on the mountain. Physically, I felt remarkably well. I had no blisters on my feet and no soreness in my legs or anywhere else. The training had really paid off in that respect.

I had prepared my muscles to take the punishment. My tendons and joints were hardened from pumping iron in the gym and going up and down the local mountains in record time. Diane and Kyle were nursing sore legs and knees, and thought that with a little more training they would have been less sapped.

But more importantly, psychologically we all felt powerful. Kilimanjaro is a huge mountain and we went to the top propelled by our fragile human bodies. No fancy machinery, short cuts or finesse, just brute strength. It made us feel like we could accomplish anything. We were ready for the next challenge in life, be it another mountain or something more civilized in our daily lives; it made no difference, we were ready.

But right now, we were on our way to a photo safari. We had just conquered the roof of Africa and gazed down on the vast continent from a unique, but distant vantage point. To experience the Dark Continent up close, we had to get into the middle of the savanna and be surrounded by natives and wild animals.

We therefore continued our African adventure by heading to one of the many game parks to immerse ourselves in the wild. We chose the Masai Mara National Game Park for this part of our tour.

Back at the hotel we waited for our ride, which true to form was over an hour late. By now we had learned about African schedules and knew what to expect. Eventually a minivan showed up and we headed to downtown Nairobi to pick up the rest of the crew.

Our driver and safari guide was a man named Moses. He appeared to be in his early forties and, unlike the guides on the mountain, obviously did not exercise much, judging by a small spare tire around his mid section. This, of course, had no effect on his ability to perform as a safari guide. It turned out he was like a walking encyclopedia once we entered the game park.

Downtown, we double-parked on a very busy commercial street. We waited as Moses sauntered into a nearby office and brought back three more Americans. The first was a young man from Canada, named Assif, who was actually born in neighboring Tanzania. He was nearing the end of his vacation and wanted to take in a few days of safari.

The others were a young couple from Pennsylvania, Stacey and Adam, who were newlyweds on the second half of their extended honeymoon. They had just left Egypt, where they toured the Great Pyramids at Giza, and were now beginning their stay in Kenya.

We were lucky to be teamed up with such a good group of people. We had a lot in common, and although Diane and I were a few years older than the rest, we could still relate to them. Again, Kyle got along well with the adults, especially with Stacey. The two of them developed a rapport that was suitable for the opening act at a comedy club and would clown with each other at every opportunity.

We were the only ones with a kid, and Moses used that fact to affectionately refer to Diane as "Safari Mama." This, of course, became her nickname for the rest of the time in Africa, and beyond.

Our drive to the Masai Mara and our photo safari took us west of Nairobi along a well-trafficked road through gently rolling hills. Suddenly, around a sharp bend in the road, the wooded terrain opened dramatically and we got a fabulous view of the Great Rift Valley.

We could see forever — the only obstruction was the light haze that hung in the air. The Great Rift Valley is a giant chasm in the earth's crust that runs from Syria to Mozambique. Part of this valley is the Olduvai Gorge, where Louis Leakey, the British anthropologist, gathered many early human fossils. His excavations, including his famous find, Lucy, an early hominoid fossil, were located in this valley.

Our van rocked us from side to side as it rolled down the serpentines of the gently sloping Rift Valley walls. Kyle pointed out a group of baboons walking along the side of the road. We turned off the paved road and lurched down a dirt road followed by a rooster tail of dust.

The ever-changing landscape unfolded like a documentary film with us as participants. We spotted zebras, wildebeest, impalas, gazelles, antelopes, giraffes, jackals, secretary birds, and vultures, all before we ever entered the game park. We observed Masai tending their herds of cattle, goats, or sheep along the road and drove past Masai villages, called bomas, consisting of several low mud huts arranged in circles and surrounded by thick thornbush fences.

One thing is certain: they do not have any building codes in Masai land. The Masai villages are very primitive. They look no better than the simple forts we built when I was ten or twelve years old, playing with my buddies in the dusty fields. Apparently, a fire was constantly burning in the center of the boma, because the air around these bomas was always hazy and irritated our noses and throats.

Kyle was astounded. As an American teenager, he absolutely could not imagine what it would be like to live with the Masai. The bomas are in the middle of nowhere. There is absolutely nothing but dry grassland around for hours.

We saw Masai kids and teenagers collecting wood and tending herds of cattle and goats. They must do other things, but we did not know what. As much as we observed them and talked to the Masai at the camp, we could not figure it out. The Masai and their lifestyle remained a real mystery to him, as well as the rest of us.

We manuevered down a rutted dirt road and pulled into camp, where Moses showed us to our accommodations. There was a series of large, stand-up tents and each one had two cots and a small, make-shift dresser. One tent was for Diane and me, Kyle shared one with Assif, and the newlyweds had their own tent.

In the camp, we could see a group of people having some

kind of celebration. This group surrounded a couple who were dressed like Masai. We found out they were an older couple from Holland, who apparently had just gotten married Masai style. They looked a bit out of place with blood-red makeup on their faces and wrapped in shukas. It seemed a little goofy, but it must have been some exotic romantic urge that brought them here.

After a late lunch, we jumped back in the van for a quick game run into the Mara. We bounced down a dirt road with deep ruts and then skidded through a small lake. Moses commented, "This is a short cut into the park, because we're running late." I thought, short cut, my foot. By sneaking in the back, he didn't have to pay the daily park fee per tourist. He or his company could make a few extra bucks.

Apparently, our driver was not as holy as his namesake was. But we had already noticed there were many levels on which to do business in Africa. Many would be considered corrupt or illegal in the United States but, according to Chris MacDonald, occurred here all the time, especially by "government officials."

Small dirt roads crisscross the entire park. Our van rolled down these narrow dirt roads as we were confronted with herds of wildebeest and Plains zebras. The wildebeest are impressive to see in large herds, which number thousands of animals.

Up close or individually they look a bit like a cross between a cow and a Great Dane. The grunts and snorts they make also sound like a cross between a moo and a bark; these strange grunts and snorts are constantly emerging from the herds.

Moses told us, "Wildebeest are migratory animals. They follow the rains and pass through the Masai Mara in August and September on their way to the Serengeti Plains in Tanzania. The zebras tag along with them." It's a spectacular sight to see such large herds of animals on the open plains.

Wildebeest as far as the eye can see.

It must be the biggest congregation of large mammals on earth. The carnivorous cats love the annual migration, because food is easy and plentiful. Within a few minutes, we saw our first superpredators. It was astonishing to see wild lions just lying by the side of the road. There were no zoo attendants to feed them or fences to confine them. They were free, doing whatever nature intended them to do, which at the moment meant resting and doing nothing.

We came upon several small herds of elephants that barely acknowledged our presence. The mothers made half-hearted attempts to shield their calves from us safari seekers, but otherwise they continued feeding and minding their own business.

We encountered impalas, elands, waterbucks, Thompson gazelles, and a lonely African Marsh Eagle sitting high in a tree. There were other vehicles that occasionally stopped, and the driv-

Any closer, we'd be flat as pancakes.

ers spoke in Swahili to each other, exchanging information about sights to keep their finicky clients captivated.

At one point, we saw a group of at least ten vehicles in the distance. We angled that way and quickly determined that a group of three female lions was downwind of a small herd of very nervous zebras. The zebras were looking in the direction of the lions with their ears straight up.

The vehicles were parked parallel to the side of the lions, which they seemed to ignore completely. None of the animals appeared to pay too much attention to the vehicles or the people in them.

The lions continued to stalk the zebras. They crouched low, barely visible above the tall grass. Their noses were high in the wind. The air was thick with tension. All of a sudden, the lions charged forward. The zebras took off as if fired from a cannon.

The herd of zebras all ran in the same direction. First it was straight away from the lions, then they veered to the right. The lions chased for a while, but not too vigorously, and this time they were unsuccessful. With all the easy prey in their backyard, they didn't want to expend too much energy on a given meal.

Daylight was fading; it was near sunset. As we drove toward the exit, we stopped and Moses spoke to another driver. Suddenly we made a ninety-degree turn down a dirt road that was so small it was just two parallel dirt lines separated by the width of a car.

Moses looked around, but didn't tell us what he had heard. We could tell by his intensity that it was something special and we wondered what it might be. Carefully, we approached a large bush, slightly elevated on a knoll. We crept closer and closer.

In the beam of the headlamps, two golden eyes lit up like flashlights. As our vision adjusted to the changing light, we saw that we were face to face with our second superpredator. It was a full-sized leopard crouched over an impala. He was pulling meat from the kill and filling his belly when he briefly sneered at us exposing his deadly fangs. He was not too nervous, even though we were maybe one car length away from him.

There were no hyenas, jackals, or vultures around. The leopard was spectacularly beautiful. His fur was soft and shiny and he looked immaculate. Leopards are seldom seen by tourists, because they are rare and keep to thick brush where they are well concealed.

Darkness engulfed the plains as we watched a while longer before we headed out of the park. At the park exit, the park rangers hassled Moses for staying in the park so long and trying to exit after dark. He had to get out of the van and spent five or ten minutes talking, or perhaps paying, his way out. This was part of the game that is played periodically between the safari companies and the game parks. After the rangers opened the gate, we returned to camp.

We had the good fortune of sitting or standing in the safari vehicle most of the time. Diane's knees and ankles were still sore, and the rest was just what the doctor ordered. The little bit of walking was on flat ground, which didn't stress her legs much. It gave her the opportunity to rest her muscles and tendons and have them start recovering from the torturous climb up the mountain.

Our safari mates were a likable young couple. Adam played the role of the newlywed husband quite well. Diane felt sorry for Stacey, as the safari accommodations were something less than romantic.

Compared to the conditions on the mountain, the camp was extravagant. But by any stretch of civilized standards, it was primitive. In their blissful state they were totally unprepared for the lack of common comforts, like running water, room service, or air conditioning.

The nights in Africa were surprisingly chilly, and Diane was particularly thankful that we had the foresight to bring our sleeping bags, not just to keep us warm, but also to keep us from coming in contact with the questionable bedding provided by the safari organizers.

Stacey and Adam didn't have that fortune and we gave them the sheets and blankets from our cots to help keep themselves warm. Of course, that didn't help them from touching the dubious linens.

The smell of a warm meal permeated the large mess hall, an open structure covered in chicken wire. By now, it was pitch black and the star-studded sky was lit up like a Las Vegas casino. We could see the bright Milky Way, the luminous band of stars visible in a clear night sky away from city lights. We had just seen thousands of wild animals, including lions and a leopard. Our camp had no perimeter barrier, such as a fence, a wall, or a mote. No self-shooting automatic machine-guns were evident.

There were just a couple of Masai warriors to guard the camp. Their weapons consisted of a rungu (which is a short wooden club with a bulbous head), a long spear, and a knife. To a Westerner this might seem horribly inadequate at first, considering there were large carnivorous cats, baboons, elephants, and all kinds of wild animals "out there."

The Masai were fascinating. These two warriors were brothers, named Joseph and Raphael Parmuat. They were modern Masai, in the sense that they had "jobs" and were not mere cattle herders.

They were both tall, slender men with chiseled features. They wore Shukas, which looked like checked tablecloths draped from their shoulders, and sandals made from cattle hide. They had an aristocratic manner, as though they were above everyday problems.

Our two Masai warriors were privileged, because they were the sons of the village chief. Perhaps that is why they chose not to be cattle herders. Joseph had the traditional stretched out Masai ear lobes, that he generally wore wrapped over the top of his ears in a comical coil. Raphael, who according to Diane was the more handsome of the two, had normal ears.

She asked Raphael, "I noticed your earlobes are not stretched. Why didn't you have your ears done Masai style?" He said, "When I was a boy I decided against cutting and stretching my ears and my father respected my unusual wish." Diane also learned that neither of them was married, which was surprising to her, because they both seemed like they would make a good catch for any Masai girl.

Raphael spoke English well, which he had learned from the safari clients at the camp. He was very bright and was reading an issue of the *Economist*, even though he had never traveled beyond the borders of Kenya or out of Masai land for that matter. We enjoyed talking to him.

He explained a little about the Masai and their customs. I asked him, "You said you're not an ordinary Masai, but a Masai warrior. How do you become a warrior?" "I became a warrior in 1993. It is a special way of life that takes several years of training and preparation. The last step is a test where the senior warrior takes the student to a remote area of the bush and drops him there alone, where he must take care of himself. This test lasts three months and the only weapons allowed are a knife, a spear, and a rungu." They spend three months alone in the wild! If they return, they graduate to become warriors. This is a great honor for them. And it is definitely a man's world here. Only Masai men can become warriors.

Kyle inquired, "Have you ever killed a lion?" "Yes, but I was not alone. I was with another warrior friend tending some cattle, when a female lion approached. We killed her with our spears." He said it as if it was less of an accomplishment, because there were two of them.

I thought to myself, those two Masai warriors with nothing but spears and rungus could not be considered to be ganging up on a lion. He didn't go into a lot of detail and certainly was not bragging, but you could tell he considered it a feat of bravery to have killed the lion. I would say most modern hunters with high-powered guns would consider themselves to be in a dangerous situation under the same circumstances. So maybe the camp was in good hands and well guarded after all, with those two Masai warriors as sentries.

That night we crawled into our sleeping bags early. Kyle was reading a book, *Into Thin Air*, by the glow of his headlamp. He thought it was fascinating. It's about a number of climbers who died on Mount Everest in one of the worst climbing seasons of the mountain. Reading about the mountain in so much detail made him curious about Everest.

Experiencing how his body responded to the thin air on Kilimanjaro and how he was able to force himself to fight to get to the top really gave him an emotional high. He had no idea he could feel that way about something as demanding as climbing a mountain. Therefore reading about Everest was intriguing, and he could relate it to something he had just experienced. He started thinking about the possibilities and wondered how old the youngest person to summit Everest was.

We slept well the first night. Friends in the States had cautioned us about the safari nights. They had told us that the nights come "alive" and that we may have trouble sleeping because of the many unusual noises occurring throughout the night. Indeed, a wide array of animal and jungle noises serenaded us, but I dozed off quickly.

Diane heard Stacey giving Adam a hard time in the tent next to ours; ". . . this camp is nothing like you described. The beds are uncomfortable. The toilets are on the edge of camp. The shower has only lukewarm water. The food is . . ." She went on and on. Occasionally we heard Raphael or Joseph walking through the camp checking things out. It was exciting being in a tent with thin cloth walls and having Masai warriors fighting off the wild animals around us.

I was vaguely aware of the moonlight slowly traversing

across the roof of our tent, when a shrill AIEEEE, AIEEEE, AIEEEE pierced the cool night air. A blood-chilling roar tore through the night a moment later, followed by a muffled shriek. By then, we were all wide awake, sitting up straight on our cots. We could only guess what happened. After we looked at each other in bewilderment we all went back to sleep, except Stacey, and by default, Adam.

In the morning we saw Joseph and Raphael and asked them about the growling. "It was a kill about one hundred meters south of camp," Joseph explained. "Can we go investigate?" I asked, and off we went. We crouched low and squeezed through some trees and bushes that surrounded the camp.

Joseph and Raphael led, and Diane, Kyle, Assif, and I followed closely. We tried to follow in their exact footsteps, because we did not want to meet up with snakes or giant bugs hiding in the grass.

Once through the bushes, we cautiously entered an open field of tall grass. We had walked no more than one minute from camp when the Masai slowed, then gestured and rapidly exchanged some words in Swahili.

We couldn't see anything unusual. Joseph said, "Look here, leopard tracks. He took down a small gazelle." He could read the faint traces in the grass as well as a book.

Nervously, we glanced down and hidden in the soft dirt we saw tracks with bloodstains in the grass. We detected the faint odor of animal feces. "Where did the leopard take its prey, and more important where is he now?" I inquired. "He took the body to that tree over there," Joseph replied, as he pointed to a group of trees along the horizon. "Leopards are shy, it's hard to find them." "As long as he doesn't find us first, it's okay. We already saw one last night, near the lake, eating an impala," I told them. With that, we headed back to the "safety" of our camp. That's an exciting part of being on safari, to learn that a leopard was hunting so close to our flimsy tents.

With this excursion behind us, we headed back into the game park. This time through the front gate, legally, instead of sneaking in the back way. We labored our way through large herds of zebra and wildebeest. The first thing we did was go back and check on where the leopard had been eating the impala the evening before. We saw no sign of the leopard.

A few large vultures were hovering in the nearby trees. A few broken bones, and the intact impala horns were scattered in the matted grass. Moses told us, "The leopard dragged the carcass up some tree and stored it, so the vultures and hyenas won't get to it. See those vultures up there, those are Egyptian vultures, and those over there are white-hooded vultures. They show up wherever there's a meal." We saw lots of vultures in the Mara; either on top of trees or soaring high above the plains catching thermal updrafts.

Moses steered our way into more open areas. He was the consummate safari guide as he pointed out animals left and right, including the rare and difficult to see. There were the adorable dik-dik (the smallest species of antelope), the unusual topi, a shy serval, a flock of guinea fowl, and chipper warthogs. You name it, he would find them and take us to them. One time, he noticed something in a large grassy field alongside a tree-lined gully.

We headed in that direction and came upon a pride of five lions bounding toward the trees. We were on a tiny dirt road, which was temporarily blocked with signs posted by the park service. Moses told us, "If we get caught here by the park rangers, there will be a hundred dollar fine." "We spent a lot of money to get here.

Kilimanjaro Adventure

What's another hundred dollars?" Adam replied. I quickly added, "We'll split it three ways. Don't worry, Moses; take us where you think we should go." That was good enough for Moses and he drove around the signs.

Ignoring us, the lions traipsed past us and disapeared into the thick brush. We cleverly proceeded down the road in the direction where they had come from. All of a sudden, we saw four more lions, two large females and two cubs, devouring a freshly killed wildebeest.

We were the only vehicle in the vicinity when we pulled up directly next to them; they barely acknowledged our presence. They continued tearing and gnawing at the carcass. The smell of fresh meat permeated the air; one clear sign they had just killed their prey. There was no cruelty about the scene — it's simply nature's way that some die so others may live.

Surprisingly there were no hyenas, jackals, or vultures. We sat and observed the mid-morning eating habits of this pride. Kyle thought it was one of the most impressive sights he had ever witnessed. Watching wild lions with no bars or motes in between was an intense feeling. He thought everyone in the world should have a chance to enjoy this. Moses kept an eye out for the park rangers, as we watched the lions. The large female moved away for a few minutes and then headed back for more.

According to Moses, she physically removed herself from the carcass, so she would not continue to stuff herself. Part of the pride had already engorged themselves to the point where they could not eat anymore. When they were all stuffed, they headed toward the shade of the trees for rest. The lions were satisfying their appetites as ours were growing.

The Keekorok Lodge is in the middle of the Masai Mara. This is a beautiful, luxurious resort, with individual huts, and an in-

A small pride of lions, two large females and two cubs, feasting on a freshly killed wildebeest.

viting swimming pool. We stopped at a group of thatched huts and enjoyed our picnic lunch, consisting of salad, potatoes, and chicken. After the snack we had refreshments at the bar, and treated Moses to his favorite drink — a German liqueur called "Jagermeister."

We continued on our discovery as we drove past a stone marker, which indicated the Kenya/Tanzania border. We arrived at the Mara River and Moses proclaimed, "Since we're no longer on the Kenyan side of the park, you can get out and walk around. But you must be careful, there are a lot of dangerous animals around here."

He wasn't kidding — we immediately noticed large baboons and a troop of rhesus monkeys scurrying between the dense bushes. Leaving the safety of our security pod created a whole new sensation, and generated an intense feeling of being part of the wild.

Just getting out of the safari van made our nerves tingle. "Do you think it's safe to be walking around with all those wild creatures? Just hearing them at night is enough for me," Stacey confided in Diane.

After having seen so many lions and how stealthy they were, Kyle figured a few could come charging out of the surrounding bushes. Even the wild baboons made him uneasy. They have huge, wicked teeth and are tough. They have been known to defend themselves with furious aggression against lions and to end up injuring the lion.

The river was teeming with hippopotamuses. Moses told us, "Hippos are the second largest land animal on earth, second only to the elephant. Remember hippos kill thousands of people in these parts of Africa, so you don't want to provoke them."

That sounded like good advice, because we were looking directly at them with nothing between them and us. No walls. No moats. Of course, we had no clue what would be considered a provocation to a wild hippo.

We saw two groups of hippos. One group was directly in front of us, bathing in the center of the murky river. It consisted of about twelve to fifteen animals. The other group of perhaps twenty hippos was farther downstream.

We were definitely in their territory. The banks of the river had deep trenches carved in them through which the hippos regularly pushed their huge bodies. Cautiously we walked through those same trenches during our excursion.

I handed the camera to Diane to take a picture of me in the foreground and the river with the hippos in the background. I walked to the edge where the water met the flat rock. Kyle was strolling along the embankment not too far from me. Suddenly, a large bull hippo in the center of the motionless river turned toward us and lunged. Half of his huge body and his thick front legs were out of the water.

His giant mouth was wide open with dagger-like teeth pointing straight at us. Water was spraying everywhere with tremendous noise as he crashed back into the water. His gaping mouth looked about as large as the open trunk of a car. He made a ferocious roar, like a jetliner during take-off.

We all took notice instantly and scattered away from the river. Especially Kyle and me, since we were closest to the water and closest to that giant mouth with the huge teeth heading our way. The hippo heaved up again, bucked and splashed, and seemed to be gaining momentum like an avalanche. The hippo was moving at incredible speed. The two lunges were separated by just a few milliseconds.

We shot up the embankment, eager to get beyond the reach of the hippo's fury. Shortly after the second lunge, I had sprinted far enough from the brown water to take a breather. I spun around to look back. The hippo was now totally submerged and I couldn't see him. As a matter of fact, all the hippos were submerged and were invisible.

Apparently, they all got scared too. I watched the deadly stream nervously and saw them break the surface of the water one by one. Then the bull hippo finally appeared toward the center of the river giving us the evil eye.

Everyone else was huddled in the van except Kyle, who was lurking behind the vehicle. Stacey was right next to him in the open door and she never got out of the van again until we were back in camp.

Even before the incident with the hippo, she didn't dare to venture too far from the open door of the van, because she thought she might turn into crocodile bait. Stacey's comment to Kyle was, "Ixnay on the savage wilderness. Maybe the hippo gods are looking for a teenage sacrifice."

Apparently, the hippo simply had to establish his territory and let us know that we were intruding. The tremendous show of hostility convinced all of us. I turned to Diane and remarked, "Tell me you got the photo with the hippo charging." "Are you crazy? I'm glad to be alive and I think I did well to still have the camera," she blustered.

She had a point. Then I learned that she did drop the camera, but fortunately, she had the strap around her neck so it didn't go far. Cautiously, I moved back to the edge of the river for the photo, but the hippos were laying low and didn't pose for another spectacular photo opportunity.

Kyle pointed across the river and exclaimed, "Look at the size of the crocodiles over there." We immediately turned our heads and noticed several huge crocodiles on the other side of the river, sunning themselves on the embankment. "It took us this long to notice them. We better be careful, there could be some on this side too," I added. By this time, we had been walking around in the area for the better part of the afternoon. We became more careful where we stepped, especially in the hippo trenches where your line of sight was extremely limited.

A powerful sense of excitement and nervousness pervaded the wild territory as we walked around, especially after the bull hippo staged his murderous attack. Seeing all the other animals had been spectacular, but we had seen them from the safety of the safari vehicle, which provided a certain distance and sense of security.

Hal at Mara river with hippos in water. A few moments before, a large bull hippo charged out of the water in a ferocious attack.

Walking in the untamed terrain of Africa gave us the nerve-tingling feeling of being out in the wild. We concluded a walking safari is clearly the most exciting way to experience the African wilderness. That is what we plan for our next safari.

After snapping some last photos, we drove back to camp. Along the way, a small snake on the side of the road caught my eye. Moses stopped and backed up. We hung out the top of the vehicle and took pictures.

It was a deadly poisonous puff adder, identifiable by the markings and the special manner of locomotion. Puff adders literally walk on their ribs. We asked Moses to get closer, but he said, "I'm afraid to get the vehicle too close to the snake, because the

Kilimanjaro Adventure

A deadly puff adder taking its time crossing the road.

reptile could crawl up one of the wheel wells and end up inside the van." We didn't argue with his reasoning.

During the drive, we noticed a large concentration of safari vehicles surrounding a small group of bushes. We got word that a cheetah was there. As we drifted closer, we saw a beautiful cheetah, nervously emerging from behind a bush. Right behind the cheetah were two small cubs. The cubs were precious and appeared to be a lot less nervous than the mother.

The cubs had darker fur than the mother and bushy, silver manes. Judging by those features and size, they might have been about six to eight weeks old. The cubs were running around playing with each other, even with all the vehicles around. The cubs ran and pounced on each other, then pounced on the mom. It was a beautiful sight, just like a scene from *Wild Discovery*.

Back at the park exit, the rangers simply waved us through

A nervous cheetah mom with her two little cubs.

this time. As we approached our camp, a young Masai boy with a shepherd's staff herded his cattle across the dirt road in front of our vehicle. We stopped and raised our cameras to take pictures, but he waived us off.

Moses cautioned us, "Many Masai still don't want to have their pictures taken. Apparently, they're superstitious about the camera and think that somehow it captures their soul." He offered to drive us to a Masai village in the morning, where we'd be able to take pictures, but for a fee.

It sounded fascinating to visit a Masai village, spend time with them, and be able to take pictures. However, we had a real conflict with the concept of supporting the sale of Masai culture for tourism. We contemplated it and decided against it. Mostly because we wouldn't be exposed to "real Masai," but to a "tourist version" of Masai.

After dinner, at the camp, we sat around the fire that our Masai warriors, Joseph and Raphael, had made. They were breaking up more wood for the fire. Joseph was thrusting the narrow, pointed end of his spear repeatedly into a large log. He did this with one hand and with great precision. After a few thrusts, large portions of firewood broke off the log.

Naturally, all the guys had to check out the spear. We took a few thrusts into the log and the ground, and were amazed at how Joseph handled the spear with such great skill. None of us could match the precision Joseph displayed.

That night a troop of screeching monkeys burst into the trees surrounding our enclave. Their chattering and cries competed with the thrashing leaves and branches in the cool air.

Back at camp. Left to right: Our cook, Gebra, Masai warrior Joseph Parmuat, Masai warrior Raphael Parmuat, Diane, Kyle, and Hal.

The pandemonium they created drowned the distant animal noises we were getting accustomed to. Fortunately, they did not dare to invade our tented camp. Like the lions and other animals, they probably had too much respect for the Masai warriors and their deadly weapons.

In the middle of the night, Diane had to use the bathroom, which was on the edge of camp. Spooked by the eerie noises, she didn't pretend to be carefree enough to venture out and risk her life just to relieve herself. It made more sense to her to wake me up so I could accompany her. In my half sleep, I wriggled out of my sleeping bag, rolled off my cot, put on some clothes, got a flashlight, and escorted her to the facilities.

To make it more fun, I teased her by leaving the tent with the flashlight off. It was too creepy for Diane and I didn't want to give her heated imagination any more fuel, so after a sharp tug on my shoulder I turned it on. In her mind we were already being stalked by vicious cats. Or perhaps Joseph and Raphael would mistake us for roaming animals and knock us over the head with their rungus.

The next morning we made further excursions through the park. I guess we didn't get enough of the huge herds and exotic animals normally found in zoos. But then it was time to return to Nairobi. Along the way, we stopped at some gift shops to pick up some mementos.

We rummaged through mountains of wood-carved animals, primitive weapons, jewelry for every imaginable body part, and other stuff displayed on modest shelves. After a lot of negotiating and haggling we bought a few things at a good price, but probably still overpaid.

At one roadside shop a stalemate developed while we negotiated for some salad spoons. The spoons were made of camel bone handles with rosewood bowls. We arrived at a dollar amount that we wouldn't exceed and the merchant was not willing to let them go. The merchant hestitated and then presented a workable solution. He wanted me to add the T-shirt I was wearing as part of the deal.

The shirt had no real value for me; it was a free T-shirt I had received from the blood bank for donating blood, so I added it to the deal. Diane's face beamed while she walked away with the spoons and I pulled another shirt from the luggage. We all laughed and made jokes about giving "the shirt off my back."

We decided to finish the trip with a nice dinner at a fancy restaurant in Nairobi. We'd heard and read about some good restaurants and chose one, which had been reviewed and touted in *Gourmet* magazine. This one is a specialty restaurant — The Carnivore.

This restaurant serves meat. Lots of it. Every type of meat imaginable. Chicken, beef, pork, lamb, and more unusual game such as antelope, impala, gazelle, hartebeest, ostrich, zebra, giraffe, and crocodile. All charbroiled on long spits in a large open pit in the center of the restaurant.

The restaurant has an established routine, where the meal starts at the same time for everyone. This is because the chefs can only keep the slabs of meat properly cooked for so long. We therefore had drinks in the wood-panelled Simba Saloon while we waited for our table.

We chatted with a young Texan couple, Bob and Janet, who were trying to rein in their precocious two-year-old. They had been living in Zaire, but had to leave due to civil unrest that unfolded when Mobutu Sese Seko, the former leader of Zaire, was overthrown in May 1997, and the rebel leader Laurent Kabila took over government powers and leadership.

Janet told us of their harrowing plight of having less than two hours to evacuate their home or face the possibility of execution by wild, roaming mobs. Later, the government forces allowed them to go back to retrieve personal belongings.

Much to their sadness, they found that their home had been looted and stripped to the bare walls. Bob said, "I even spotted a couple of thugs wearing our clothes. But I didn't dare confront them." We felt so sorry for them as they also recounted several stories of family heirlooms that were lost.

You could see the sadness in their faces as they told their stories. Diane asked them, "What are you going to do now?" Janet said, "We're going to stay here." Apparently, Bob's employer was looking for a safe place for them to live, so he could continue to fulfill his contract obligations.

All in all, they told us that they liked living in Africa. We got the feeling that this continent can get a hold of you in this way. Then the routine for the feast commenced.

The aroma of fresh-barbequed meat permeated the hot pit, and as we walked to our table our mouths began to salivate like Pavlovian dogs. Waiters walked by the tables and sliced slabs of meat off the spits onto our plates. "I have gazelle meat for you this time. I recommend a touch of the masala sauce with it," a young waiter said.

A Lazy Susan with garlic, chimichurri, sweet and sour, masala, mint, and chili sauces occupied the center of the table. We breathed deeply to savor the spicy scent vaporizing from the hot fare and took pleasure in dining on perfectly roasted exotic meats. They just kept coming back with all the various types of meat until we gave them the signal to stop serving. All three of us agreed that the zebra and ostrich meats were particularly good. A perfect way to crown a perfect adventure.

The next morning we packed up our stockpile of climbing and safari gear, our personal effects, our African loot, and headed for home. As we were leaving we all reflected on this great family adventure.

Apparently, we had to travel all the way to Africa and climb the tallest mountain on the continent to help bring us closer together, not as parents and a child, but as friends. Indeed, we had journeyed to the kind embrace of victory.

Appendix I

Travel Information

There are a lot of companies that can help you plan and organize expeditions to Kilimanjaro and safaris in Africa. The services of these companies range from obtaining permits and mandatory guides for the mountain to all-inclusive, luxury tours. We list a small sampling of these companies here for your convenience. We booked through Kilimanjaro Adventure Travel and had good success at good value. We have no experience with any of the other full-service companies and therefore cannot recommend or endorse any of these.

Full-Service Companies:

1. Kilimanjaro Adventure Travel
   1770 Massachusetts Ave., Suite 192
   Cambridge, MA 02140 - USA
   Tel: (617)868-0743, Fax: (617)497-5254
   e-mail: bookings@kilimanjaro.com
   Web site: http://www.kilimanjaro.com

2. Thompson Safaris
   347 Broadway
   Cambridge, MA 02139 - USA
   Tel: (617)876-7314, Fax: (617)497-3911
   e-mail: tsafari@aol.com
   Web site: http://www.gorp.com/thomson

3. Mountain Travel, Sobek
   6420 Fairmount Ave.
   El Cerrito, CA - USA
   Tel: (510)527-8100, (800)227-2384
   Fax: (510)525-7710
   e-mail: info@MTsobek.com
   Web site: http://www.mtsobek.com

4. Mountain Madness
   4218 S. W. Alaska St., #206
   Seattle, WA 98116 - USA
   Tel: (206)937-8389, (800)328-5925
   Fax: (206)937-1772
   e-mail: mountmad@aol.com
   Web site: http://www.mountainmadness.com

5. American Alpine Institute, Ltd.
   1515 - 12th Street
   Bellingham, WA 98225 - USA
   Tel: (360)671-1505

6. Rafiki Africa
   P.O. Box 76400
   Nairobi, Kenya

Tel/Fax: (254-2)884-238
e-mail: safarico@arcc.or.ke

7. Zara Tanzania Adventures
P.O. Box 1990
Moshi, Tanzania
Tel: 255-55-54240/50808
Fax: 255-55-53105/50233
e-mail: zara@form-net.com

For people who prefer to organize the expeditions themselves, the following information is useful. A permit and local guides are compulsory and are available at the park gate, but it is recommended that they be obtained at least a week in advance since only 50 permits per day are available. A park fee is required and in 1997 was approximately $200 per person for a five day visit on the Marangu trail, and approximately $300 per person for other routes. The permits can be obtained directly through the National Park. Also, the last two companies listed, Rafiki Africa and Zara Tanzania Adventures, are local companies. They are familiar with all the local requirements and customs and can provide any level of assistance requested.

Kilimanjaro National Park
P.O. Box 96
Marangu, Tanzania
Tel: Marangu 50

Other useful information for self-organizers can be obtained from the following:

1. Kilimanjaro Mountain Club
   P.O. Box 66
   Moshi, Tanzania

2. Mountain Club of Kenya
   P.O. Box 45741
   Nairobi, Kenya
   Tel: 501747

3. Tanzania National Parks
   P.O. Box 3134
   Arusha, Tanzania

Local hotels and hostels:

1. Marangu Hotel
   P.O. Box 40
   Moshi, Tanzania
   Tel: Marangu 11

2. Kibo Hotel
   P.O. Box 102
   Marangu, Tanzania
   Tel: Marangu 4

3. The Moshi Hotel
   P.O. Box 1369
   Arusha, Tanzania

4. YMCA
   Moshi and Arusha

Local transportation can be arranged via rental car or through shuttle services:

1. Davanu Shuttle Service
   Windsor House, 4th Floor, University Way
   P.O. Box 9081
   Nairobi, Kenya
   Tel: (254-2)222002/217178

2. Orion Tours and Travel, Ltd.
   Corner House, 10th Floor, Kimathi St.
   Nairobi, Kenya
   Tel: 22-11-28

3. Pinnacle Tours and Travel, Ltd.
   Am Bank House. Lower Gr. Flr., Uni. Way
   Nairobi, Kenya
   Tel: 33-54-72

A valid passport is required, as are entry visas for Tanzania and Kenya, if your travels go through Kenya. They can be obtained in advance at the following addresses:

1. Tanzania Embassy
   2139 R Street NW
   Washington, DC 20008
   Tel: (202)939-6125

2. Kenya Embassy
   2249 R Street NW

Washington, DC 20008
Tel: (202)387-6101

There are literally hundreds of companies that can arrange for tours and safaris in the national game parks with little or no advance notice. There is a wide variety of safaris, including driving, camping, walking, camel, and balloon rides. One of the larger, more diversified safari companies is United Touring Company. They have several offices in Africa:

1. United Touring Company
   Muindi Mbingu/Kaunda St.
   P.O. Box 42196
   Nairobi, Kenya
   Tel: (254-2)33-19-20
   Fax: (254-2)33-14-22

2. United Touring Company
   Subzali Bldg, Goliondoi Rd.
   P.O. Box 2211
   Arusha, Tanzania
   Tel: (255-57)8844/5
   Fax: (255-57)8222

3. United Touring Company
   United House, 4 Park Street
   P.O. Box 2914
   Harare, Zimbabwe
   Tel: (263-4)793701
   Fax: (263-4)792794

4. United Touring Company
P.O. Box 50029
Victoria & Alfred Waterfront
Cape Town, South Africa
Tel: (27-21)419-8301
Fax: (27-21)419-2422

We will list a few other companies that operate out of Nairobi for your convenience:

1. Across Africa Safaris, Ltd.
Bruce House, 4th Floor
Standard St.
Nairobi, Kenya
Tel: 33-27-44

2. Big Safari Service, Ltd.
Siloma House, 1st Floor
Koinage St.
Nairobi, Kenya
Tel: 33-97-56

3. Bunson Safaris
P.O. Box 45456
Standard St.
Nairobi, Kenya
Tel: 22-29-92
Fax: 21-41-20
e-mail: bunson@form-net.com

4. Inside Africa Safaris
   Autorama Corner
   Haile Selassie Ave.
   Nairobi, Kenya
   Tel: 22-33-04

5. Perry Mason Safaris, Ltd.
   P.O. Box 49655
   Nairobi, Kenya
   Tel: 88 23 49
   Fax: 88 43 12

6. Rhino Safaris, Ltd.
   Nairobi Hilton Arc
   City Hall Way
   Nairobi, Kenya
   Tel: 22 81 02

7. Safari Camp Services, Ltd.
   Nginyo House
   Koinage St.
   Nairobi, Kenya
   Tel: 22 89 36

8. Safari Seekers, Ltd.
   P.O. Box 9165
   Nairobi, Kenya
   Tel: 24-14-08

9. Savorsen Safaris
   Fairlane House, 4th Floor
   Mbagathi Rd.
   Nairobi, Kenya
   Tel: 72-56-30

10. Sekai Kenya, Ltd.
    Cianda House, 1st Floor
    Koinange St.
    Nairobi, Kenya
    Tel: 21-29-69

11. Simba Safaris Co.
    Hilton Hotel Bldg
    Simba St.
    Nairobi, Kenya
    Tel: 33-84-00

12. Tropical Nature & Cultural Safaris
    Jubilee Exchange, 4th Floor
    Mama Ngina St.
    Nairobi, Kenya
    Tel: 22-53-63

13. Universal Safari Tours, Ltd.
    Cotts House
    Wabera St.
    Nairobi, Kenya
    Tel: 22-14-46

14. White Lion Safaris, Ltd.
    P.O. Box 61542
    Nairobi, Kenya
    Tel: 21-57-91

15. Wild Kingdom Safaris, Ltd.
    Rehema House, 4th Floor
    Standard St.
    Nairobi, Kenya
    Tel: 22-69-60

Appendix II

Testimonials

The Internet is a great resource, but we were cautious about dealing with a company that we knew nothing about and had just plucked out of the ether. There has been a lot of news about scams and fly-by-night companies on the Internet. To verify that we were dealing with a reputable company, we asked for a list of references and former clients, which was promptly forwarded to us.

We contacted everyone on the list and asked for their experience with the company and any feedback or tips about Africa. It turned out that everyone had a good experience with the company, but more important, they all gave some detail about their own experiences in Africa. Their responses helped us plan our trip and provided some useful tips and an excellent account of other destinations. Excerpts of some of the messages are provided in this appendix.

Hello Hal and Diane:

My son, daughter and I went on a photo safari and I can't overstate that we had the best time ever on a trip. Our tour was probably different from the one you are planning, but Kilimanjaro

Adventure Travel can certainly arrange the things you are interested in seeing and doing. My son and daughter are 32 and 35 and we mostly wanted to see wild animals, but also wanted to experience some of the local atmosphere. She booked a guide who was able to give us a private safari where we stayed in a makeshift camp in the bush.

Our camp consisted of private tents instead of one of the many camping areas or lodges that are located in the game parks. When I was at the San Diego Wild Animal Park a few years ago, I stayed in tents and I didn't want to duplicate the arrangements I could get there.

We booked our plane trips through our travel agent and spent a couple days with my daughter in New Orleans before leaving for Kenya. Our British Airway connections went through New York and then to London and then directly to Nairobi, all without problems.

We arrived in the evening and we stayed one night at a Kenya hotel before we took off again. This really is required. On the return trip, we spent another night in Nairobi. Since we had only had one cold shower in two weeks, it was necessary just to get back to civilization.

Nairobi is at an altitude of over 1000 meters and when you go to Kilimanjaro you'll be much higher. The temperatures are much cooler than we expected for being right on the equator. Most of the time I wore long sleeve shirts and, in the evenings, a jacket or a sweater.

I enjoy camping, but I like to have good meals. We had great meals on our safari, which were cooked on a campfire by a chef who used to work at a Nairobi restaurant. None of us became ill or lost weight, which would not have hurt any of us.

I suggest you get in direct contact with your safari guide,

even though Kilimanjaro Adventure Travel provides good service. That way you can avoid any communication problems that might otherwise occur. Most of the time the guides will be out of the office on safari, but many will have an e-mail address and can be contacted. If you start planning early enough you can line up everything you want to do.

Please let me know if you have other questions. I'm 59 and could be in better shape, but I did at least as well as my younger son. When you're in a game area you don't do a lot of walking. I don't know about Kilimanjaro, but I imagine you have to be in pretty good shape. I have friends who climbed it several years ago and they did well and camped out without any problems.

Good luck, Jack

Dear Hal:

My boyfriend and I had a fabulous time on Kilimanjaro and Stephanie did a good job making all the arrangements. She simply makes the bookings from her office and you could plan the whole trip without her. You can contact everyone yourself and save the middleman. I would be glad to provide you with the names and numbers of all the people I dealt with.

The first day we stayed in a cheap hotel in Nairobi. We were on a budget and could not spend too much money. I guess there are basically two types of hotels in Nairobi, both cheap and simple or expensive and nice with not much in between. Nairobi is a strange and scary place and I did not dare do any sight seeing or anything.

The next morning we were waiting for the bus, which did

not show up at the scheduled time, so I went to call Rafiki with no luck. Then I really became concerned, but finally about forty-five minutes later it showed up. That was really the only time I was worried that the plans weren't working out. We took the bus to Arusha and then on to Moshi.

We stayed at the Green Cottage in Moshi and had no idea how we would start climbing the next day. I called Zara International to tell them that we had arrived in Moshi and they made arrangements to pick us up the next morning and take us to the mountain.

We took the Machame route, which is really beautiful. We camped in tents that they provided and the porters carried and pitched. We rented sleeping bags and Thermo-rest pads. The sleeping bags were fine, but I would have preferred to have my own. The food was not bad. They fixed a variety of dishes and gave us plenty of everything, but take plenty of powerbars and granola bars and that kind of stuff. You will really miss the taste of home food.

Our guide and assistant guide were excellent. Our guide's name was Brycan Mandari and the assistant guide was Thomas. We had walking poles, which I highly recommend.

We went on a three day safari and that was plenty. You will see all the animals in the first three hours of the safari. I could go on and on about the great time we had, so let me know if there is anything else.

Bye, Rebecca

Hello Hal, Diane, and Kyle

My wife and I went on a safari in Kenya last June and then also took a side trip to an animal hospital. Stephanie made all the arrangements for us, including the domestic Kenya flights. We were pleasantly surprised with all the arrangements she made for us. When we arrived in Kenya her partner called us at our hotel to see if we needed anything. Everything went as planned and we had a very smooth trip and a good time.

We never went to climb Mt. Kilimanjaro, so I can't say anything about that part of the trip. We stayed in Kenya the whole time we were in Africa. We booked a safari through Safari Camp Services and had a wonderful time. The food was very good; so were the guides and the camps in the parks. Our camp consisted of large tents.

You will see really bad roads, but since you're not in your own car you get used to them. It's a good idea to take some really good anti-diarrhea medicine. Nairobi isn't the greatest place, but if you stay close to your hotel you should be fine. There are plenty of taxis and they are very reliable, but negotiate the fare before you get in, so you won't get ripped off.

Let me know if you have any more questions. I wish you a great trip.

Sincerely, Mark

Hello Hal,

Stephanie organized my trip and hooked me up with Rafiki in Nairobi. They did a good job. Rafiki planned everything once I got to Nairobi. The bus ride from Nairobi to Moshi went well on the way down.

But there was a four hour delay in Arusha on the way

back. We had to transfer buses at the border and there was a problem with the bus that was supposed to pick us up. So to make a long story short, make sure you build in extra time for the bus rides, especially if you are trying to catch a flight.

The other thing, there are plenty of con artists just waiting at the border to talk you into buying stuff. One guy noticed that I was from the US and he said: "You're an American...follow me." I knew I only had to get my passport stamped at this border crossing. He was trying to get me to go in the direction away from the passport office.

So be alert, especially when you're at the border! I recommend that you check out the US travel advisories on the Internet. If you're traveling in a big group you'll be OK.

Take as much time as possible to climb up Kili, at least 6 days or more. We pushed up in 5 days last summer and my lungs have never fully recovered.

Just 8 months before going to Kili I had trekked to Base Camp of Mt. Everest, which is at about the same altitude and I had no problems, but it took over 15 days. Six days is simply not enough time to get acclimatized and to climb up Kili, but you don't have much choice.

The mountain guides are really pushy for a tip and they will remind you how much they want during the climb. It's a good idea to have the exact change to tip each porter and the guides. Figure on a $100.00 split among all of them.

Make sure you carry the exact change in smaller bills with you. They are notorious for not having change for tourists; i.e. have a 100 shilling bill when needed, rather than a 200 shilling bill. Seeing the animals was fantastic and the scenery was spectacular. You'll love every moment of your visit.

Have fun, Heather

Kilimanjaro Adventure

Dear Hal:

We organized a tour with Stephanie Hancock's assistance and my wife and I had a wonderful time in Africa. She was a big help in picking out local operators for our Kilimanjaro climb and for our safari, including hotels and accommodations. All the accommodations worked out well. We especially liked the Kirurumu Tented Lodge.

We also stayed at the Ilburu Lodge, which was very beautiful and the accommodations were okay. If this lodge had better showers it would have made quite a difference. Zara Tours, which organized the Kilimanjaro climb, were very professional. Hoopoe Adventure Tours took us on the safari and they did a fine job also.

They all spoke English reasonably well. Despite ample warnings from everyone we had talked with ahead of time, none of us on the trip had any problems with the food or water. We always had a good feeling that they were taking good care of us. The only time we felt uneasy is when a herd of elephants started getting aggressive and trumpeting at us.

And one other time when a pride of lions was outside our tent one morning hunting. But, that's the difference between being in East Africa and watching Wild Discovery on TV. You can't get away from it by just changing the channel. Actually, the risk with the lions was not really that great.

The only problems we had were because of the poor telephone system in Tanzania. There are two solutions to this problem:
1) we could have altered our plans as we went and not worry about what might or might not have been arranged for us.
Or 2) we could have arranged everything before leaving the US. Point 2 would have been less stressful, but given how hectic it was

for us before the trip, it was impossible.

To summarize, plan as best you can. But be prepared to change the plans if the need arises. Do not spend a lot of time or money trying to make phone calls within Africa. And most importantly keep your sense of humor.

We had no idea what to expect from the operators when we arrived in Africa. We didn't even know that there would be several different operators handling different parts of our trip. All we knew was where we had to be and when, but we did not have the names and numbers for the contacts of the different organizations that we hoped would be waiting for us.

Importantly without fail they were waiting for us. But there was always a little anxiety that maybe nobody would be there waiting. And at the Kenya-Tanzania border crossing it would have been especially helpful to know the names of the operators we were going to contact for the next leg of the tour.

The border was a little chaotic and knowing a little more would have been useful. We had the Lonely Planet Guidebook with us, but we were still surprised a little by the lack of organization and the number of scam artists and so on.

You'll have to get off the bus and walk into an office to get your passport stamped and answer questions. After you exit, there is a good chance that your bus moved to a different spot. Since all the buses look alike, be sure to find some obvious features on your bus. Maybe some writing on the bus or certain pieces of luggage on top. It's difficult to read the dirty license plates. And if you look like you are lost, the scam artists will descend on you like piranhas.

The Masai women will hover around your wife and try to put necklaces over her head. It is OK if you want to buy a necklace, but they do pretty aggressive sales and you need to maintain control of the procedure. It helps to know what you want to buy.

Kilimanjaro Adventure

Also, there are very few collectable or unique pieces. You can buy the same stuff they sell at the border at any merchandise stand, including at the Nairobi airport.

Avoid the Hilton when you stay in Nairobi, because it's a terrible place. It is overpriced, dark, and ugly. It is a typical example of 1960s architecture, "inspired" by third world socialist functionalism.

You can stay at the Serena Lodge in Nairobi, which is relatively new, beautiful, with great service for about the same cost. Or you can stay at the Norfolk Lodge, which is this old, classic place near the University where the bus terminal is for the ride to Kilimanjaro. The Intercontinental is also acceptable.

We spent a lot of money on lodging in Nairobi when we first arrived because we did not know any better. We spent a lot of money on the way out because we wanted good service and a real shower with plentiful hot water. We spent about $ 160 per night in Nairobi and I'm sure it must be possible to get good accommodations for less than that.

We sure were thankful for the showers at Kirurumu. At the Ilburu Lodge the showers had low pressure and lukewarm water. We spent the night at the Springland, the day before the climb. The grounds were well kept and the food was great. The beds were comfortable and they had showers, but you could never get the temperature right.

The food was surprisingly good everywhere, even on the mountain. We were really worried, because my wife is a vegetarian. But they had no problem preparing good meals for her and making sure she had enough food.

We went off the beaten track for our safari to a place called Empakai Crater. It is about 80 km away from Ngoro Ngoro crater. It did not look like we had to cover much ground on a map, but on Tanzanian roads it was quite a trek. Then it rained and that slowed us down. At one point we had to get out and push and then to top it off we broke the suspension of the Land Rover.

But the whole event was beautiful. If you go to Empakai plan for two days, not just one. After you arrive, you want to hike down and spend the night. Then you can hike out the next day.

We saw a half a million flamingos, water buffalo and tracks of leopards and other predators. Since only a few groups a week go to Empakai, it is very different from some of the other places where there are so many vehicles it feels like a zoo. Of course, it all depends on what you are looking for.

There are several trails up Kilimanjaro. The most commonly used one is the Marangu route, is the least scenic and has the lowest success rate. It is by far the most crowded and therefore has the most trash. Depending on whom you read, only 30 to 40 percent of the people who ascend that route make the summit.

We took the Machame Route, which takes an extra day and has a 95 percent success rate. According to the guidebooks and the managing director of the tour company it is also the most scenic. Because it is one day longer and a little more strenuous, it is less traveled and less littered.

If you travel in a large group, the social experience may become as important as the mountain. We went in a group of four, plus our guide, an assistant guide, and several porters. It was nice to be in a small group. All I can say is that Kilimanjaro really is a magical place.

It is extremely cold at the top of Kilimanjaro and insulation does not solve the problem completely. If you think about it from a biological perspective, and understand that your body generates heat by oxidizing glucose, you have to consider what happens when there is not a lot of oxygen like at 5895 meters. That's right - you don't generate a lot of body heat.

Do not wear cotton on the final ascent. Definitely go high tech on all your undergarments, like polypropylene. The key to staying warm will be to have multiple layers of dry clothing, especially socks. Take at least two pair of dry socks for the final ascent to Uhuru Peak. All of our feet got wet and then they got cold inside our boots.

Those carbon foot warmers that you can find for skiing were helpful at first, until our feet got wet. It was not a lot of fun after that. My wife had initial stages of hypothermia. Face masks and balaclavas can help. Gatorade and other powdered drinks were great. Powerbars are useless because they were too cold and hard to eat. The soft granola bars worked well because they did not get hard. Don't underestimate the amount of snack food you can eat on a Kili climb. We had left-overs, but we were glad we had a variety and an abundant supply.

I hope you have fun on your trip. I recommend Kodak film instead of Fuji, because of the bright light, the colors work out better. Also, take lots of zip lock bags of all sizes. Learn a few words and phrases in Swahili. It is spoken through most of the region. That's all. When you get back, let me know how you trip went.

>   Best wishes.
>   Peter

Hal, Diane, and Kyle,

I went to Africa last year. I took the trucks to Lake Turkana, and then on to a seven day hike through the semi-desert with a camel train. Riding a camel for a week sure is an experience.

I am envious of you! I know that you're going to have a great time. For starters, I don't think K.A.T. organizes the trips themselves. They simply set up the contacts between the clients and the actual companies that do the organizing.

Your organizing companies will most likely be different from mine, your experience will probably also be different. But I'll tell you what happened to me and you can take it from there.

I stayed pretty much on a low budget; and that is what I wanted. I arranged for my own transportation to the company that handled my trip, Safari Camp Services. I also arranged for the accommodations before and after the safari.

On our way to Lake Turkana we slept in tents. We actually had to pitch them ourselves. Once we were in the desert we used only mosquito nets. Safari Camp Services cooked the food. It wasn't great, but it was edible and healthy. Lots of salads, porridge and stuff like that.

Most everything was very basic and simple, but nothing about the trip was really bad. You had to know ahead of time that you were going to have primitive cold showers and even more primitive toilets. Take your own toilet paper. The trucks were pretty bad and a little annoying. But after all, this is Africa.

Because Kilimanjaro is more popular I'm sure conditions are much better, but you have to remember that you are in Africa. I've only been to South and East Africa. I live in Morocco and I usually only see the westernized way of life here.

I am pretty happy with the efficiency with which things are done here, but many people who have been to the States and Europe come back appalled at how bad our services are. This includes transportation and how friendly, or unfriendly the sales people are in the stores. So things that I don't even notice might irritate you.

Kilimanjaro Adventure

Specific things I can think of quickly: you need to be careful of malaria medication, especially Lariam. Check it out before the trip on a trial basis, to see whether it bothers you. Some people think that malaria pills should not be used, but you have to remember that malaria does kill.

Absolutely do not drink the tap water in Nairobi, or any other remote places. Only uniformed tourists even try the water. I don't know how much this is due to hysteria, but it isn't nice to have the runs on a long trip. So stick will bottled water, it's a little more trouble and cost, but well worth it.

That is all I can think of right now without going into a long nostalgic trip down memory lane, under the guise of providing you with tips. :-)

Bye,

Tracey

Hi Hal:

Stephanie did a good job for us. Unfortunately, she cannot always guarantee how the local tour groups will perform on a particular trip. And the political situation that will exist at that time is out of her control.

We went on a Gorilla Safari near Lake Victoria that took us through Kenya, Tanzania, and Uganda. The trip turned out to be a wonderful experience. But true to form in Africa, not all the plans worked out properly.

The roads and service everywhere were terrible. We traveled over 1500 miles in 2 weeks. Since you are planning to climb

Kilimanjaro, our experience might not be of much help.

The political situations in Uganda and Kenya were anything but stable while we were there. We had a couple of incidents that were a little scary.

On the way to the airport in Nairobi we had to drive through a student riot. Also, six civilian cars were ambushed at the gate of Queen Elizabeth Park in Uganda the day before we arrived. It all worked out, because nobody was there and we had the park completely to ourselves!

Take care, Mike

Hal -

We flew to Nairobi on KLM with a couple of friends last June. Nairobi is a pleasant third world city with lots of activities and excitement.

We went on a safari with Savage Wilderness Travel. I spoke with the owner, Mark Savage a few days before our trip and found out some of our plans had to be changed because our guide was sick.

When we arrived, everything was chaotic and we had to take a public bus to Tanzania. Our private Land Rover ride fell through. The bus ride was okay, but we had paid for a something better.

When we arrived in Moshi there was more confusion, but we eventually arrived at the correct hotel. The next morning we met our local guide and started our five day ascent to the peak. It was a memorable experience, but only two of us actually reached the summit.

The others had to turn back due to altitude problems. We think with a better guide more of us would have made it. Our guide was good, with over seventy summit bids, but his English was poor and that made for some complications.

The climb to Uhuru Peak is not hard, if you go very slowly and everyone is reasonably fit. The more time you take to reach the summit, the greater your probability of success. Diamox works wonders and could make the difference between reaching the summit or getting altitude sickness.

I recommend taking it, because you cannot predict altitude sickness. The most experienced climber in our group had summited many 3 - 4000 meter mountains, but could not continue beyond 5000 m. The fittest and youngest climber in our group did not make it beyond 5500 m. At age 36, I was the oldest in our group of 22, and had the least altitude experience. Even so I had few problems with altitude.

The great majority of climbers on Kilimanjaro take the Marangu Route. I heard that this route is crowded and boring. And the real summit, Uhuru Peak, is another four hour hike from Gillman's Point.

Very few climbers make it past Gillman's to the real summit. But the good thing is, this route has comfortable huts and if you need help, there are plenty of other people around. We took the Maweka Route, which is more scenic, and descended along the Marangu Route.

It had been ten days between us and the last party to use these routes. There are other routes that are even more technical. I would take a more scenic and less traveled route that is compatible with everyone's abilities.

As far as safaris go, you need at least five to eight days, depending on how much money and time you have. One guy in my group stayed on for a few more days and had a great time.

There is no need to book a safari ahead of time; you can make all the arrangements in Nairobi. And it is cheaper than doing it from the US. There is so much competition for safaris that you can work out anything you want and then shop around. It is really easy. You can either do it over the phone, or go downtown Nairobi and stop in any of dozens of safari tour operators.

Stephanie Hancock was very good to work with. She even refunded some of our money because of the situation with the private ride vs. the public bus and it wasn't even her fault.

One last comment from me: climbing Kilimanjaro and going on a tour of the Tanzanian and Kenyan National Parks are world class experiences that you will never forget.

Happy climbing,

John

Hi,

I was in the Andes climbing Aconcagua and only returned yesterday, which explains why I am just now able to reply to your e-mail.

The itinerary for our African trip consisted of climbing Kilimanjaro followed by a safari with Inside Africa Safaris. The safari was excellent and I recommend it as a good way to recover from the climb.

After the safari we took a side trip to Dar Es Salam on our own and enjoyed just relaxing and not doing anything. Stephanie at Kilimanjaro Adventure Travel organized the Kili climb and safari.

All the arrangements she made were OK and everything

Kilimanjaro Adventure

went according to plan with no problems. The Kili climb along the Machame route was handled by Zara Travel Agency. They know what they are doing and they know how to make all the arrangements, including all the procedures, permits, etc. If you use the same company, please give our regards to Zainab, the manager.

We took an open bus for our safari, which is nothing but a truck that is adapted for hauling people. There were only ten travelers in the truck and we were pretty comfortable.

We saw a lot of people traveling in jeep or safari vans, it looked a little cramped and we did not envy them. Our driver and guide was named Baturo. He knew the Masai Mara and Amboselli reservations very well and we saw a lot of animals.

>Hope this is useful to you.
>Regards, Bill.

Appendix III

Equipment List

Mountaineering is loaded with rewards and privileges, but also demands and responsibilities. Responsibilities are to the individual, the team, and the environment. All the equipment required for comfort, success, and survival in the mountains has to be packed and carried. Therefore, it is important to have the proper equipment for all conditions likely to be encountered on the mountain. In stable weather, Kilimanjaro can be climbed with relatively modest equipment. On the final ascent up the crater pyramid (above Kibo hut on the Marangu route), severe cold will be encountered and proper equipment is a must. If rain sets in anywhere on the trail, hypothermia and death can occur quickly.

On Kilimanjaro, porters are available. It is best to pack your equipment in soft luggage or duffel bags, because the porters prefer to carry the loads on their heads. All gear should be put inside plastic bags (e.g., trash can liners) to keep it dry in case it rains. Climbers should always carry basic items, including sun screen, rain gear, light jacket, flashlight, food, water, and a first aid kit. The final summit attempt is performed without porters and a complete daypack is required. Wool and cotton fabrics should be avoided. The new high-tech materials, like polypropylene and other synthetics are lighter, warmer, and dry quicker.

Below is an equipment checklist for a dry-season climb:

Footwear

- ☐ Mountain boots
- ☐ Liner socks
- ☐ Socks
- ☐ Gaiters
- ☐ Sneakers (for camp)
- ☐ Crampons (not required on Marangu route)

Clothing

- ☐ Shorts
- ☐ Thermal underwear
- ☐ Hiking pants
- ☐ Polypro shirt
- ☐ Light shirt
- ☐ Heavy shirt
- ☐ Jacket
- ☐ Gloves, mittens
- ☐ Glove/mitten shells
- ☐ Hat
- ☐ Balaclava
- ☐ Visor, sun hat

Personal Gear

- ☐ Backpack
- ☐ Sleeping bag
- ☐ Sleeping pad (not required on Marangu route)
- ☐ Sun screen/lip balm
- ☐ Watch
- ☐ Map & compass
- ☐ Bug off
- ☐ Lariam (do not use above 3000 meters)
- ☐ Diamox
- ☐ Glacier glasses
- ☐ Water bottles (1 liter)
- ☐ Water purifier
- ☐ Drink mix
- ☐ Snacks
- ☐ First aid kit
- ☐ Headlamp/flashlight
- ☐ Toilet paper
- ☐ Plastic bags
- ☐ Toiletries/wash kit
- ☐ Cup/spoon
- ☐ Camera
- ☐ Book

Appendix IV

Measurements

Atmospheric pressure changes with altitude. The higher you climb the less pressure there is and therefore the less oxygen is available for breathing. You can calculate the approximate pressure for a given altitude according to the simple formula:

$$P = (0.999875)^A$$

where P equals pressure, in atmospheres, and A equals altitude, in meters. The table below shows the decrease in pressure with altitude.

Altitude (meters)	**Pressure** (atmospheres)	**Locations** (examples)
0	1.0	Sea level
1000	0.88	Lubbock, TX
2000	0.78	Santa Fe, NM
3000	0.69	Mt. San Jacinto, CA
4000	0.61	Mt. Whitney, CA
5000	0.53	Pico Bolivar, Venezuela

6000	0.47	Kilimanjaro, Tanzania
7000	0.42	Aconcagua, Argentina
8000	0.36	Xixabangma, China/ Nepal
9000	0.33	Mt. Everest, Nepal/ Tibet

Metric conversions:

Multiply meters by 3.2808 to obtain feet.

Meters	Feet
1000	3281
2000	6562
3000	9842
4000	13124
5000	16404
6000	19686
7000	22966
8000	26246
9000	29527

Multiply kilometers by 0.621 to obtain miles.

Divide feet by 3.2808 to obtain meters.

Feet	Meters
3000	914
6000	1829
9000	2743
12000	3658
15000	4572
18000	5486
21000	6401
24000	7315
27000	8230
30000	9144

Multiply miles by 1.61 to obtain kilometers.

Acknowledgments

I am indebted to Eleanor Garner for reviewing the early drafts of the manuscript and providing invaluable advice and commentary that helped me to focus the story line. This book could not have been written without her. Also, to Dr. Larry Woolf, who had the same chore of struggling through an early draft and making numerous constructive comments.

Special thanks to Lynda Kennedy for her substantive editing, and to Kathy Wittert, who skillfully performed the final editing; to Jill Masterton for assistance with the book layout; to Stephanie Hall and Anja Ludewig for the artistic cover design; and to Tom Tamoria for creating the Kilimanjaro National Park map. Without their expertise and hard work, this book would not have become a reality.

Particular gratitude goes to Timothy Keating and Pierre Schmidt for teaching us mountaineering skills necessary for the enjoyment of the mountains. And my parents, who took me on family outings at a young age and instilled an appreciation of nature and the mountains.

Additionally, I would like to recognize Bill and Kent Hinckley, Gary Smith, Pat Hall, Sigrid Hughes, Wes Baugh, Mark Friedman, Susie Kim, Yvan Dionne, John Podolsky, Phil and Paula Stoffer, Tim and Katie Lerive, and Roko and Annie Bujas for support during the training phase of our expedition.

In compiling this book, I received extensive assistance from numerous people, including Michael Kelsey, Virginia Degutis, and the published works of Dan Poynter. I would also like to thank Tim

O'Hara and Steve McDonald for presenting our story to the community in their newspaper articles. I benefited from the significant contributions made by Pete Schoening, Frank Zane, and Wally Schirra.

Last, but not least, thanks to my wife, Diane, who was responsible for the book design, helped with numerous chores associated with this project, and is always there for me. And our son, Kyle, who added something special to the whole adventure.

Bibliography

Bass, Dick; Wells, Frank; Ridgeway, Rick. *Seven Summits*. New York, NY: Warner Books, 1986.

Alighieri, Dante. *Inferno*. London, England: Penguin Books, 1949.

Bentsen, Cheryl. *Maasai Days*. New York, NY: Summit Books, 1989.

Crofts, Marylee. *Tanzania*. Minneapolis, MN: Lerner Publications Co., 1989.

Hanby, Jeanette. *Kilimanjaro National Park*. Arusha, Tanzania: Tanzania Litho Limited, 1987.

Hemingway, Ernest. *The Snows of Kilimanjaro*. New York, NY: Simon & Schuster, 1936.

Houston, Charles. *Mountain Sickness*. Scientific American, October 1992.

Kelsey, Michael. *Guide to the Worlds Mountains*. Provo, UT: Kelsey Publishing, 1990.

Krakauer, Jon. *Into Thin Air*. New York, NY: Villard Books, 1997.

Lange, Harald. *Kilimanjaro - The White Roof of Africa.* Seattle, WA: The Mountaineers, 1982.

Maren, Michael. *The Land and People of Kenya.* New York, NY: J. B. Lippincott, 1989.

Pasternak, Boris. *Doctor Zhivago.* New York, NY: Pantheon Books, 1958.

Reader, John. *Kilimanjaro.* New York, NY: Universe Books, 1982.

Stahl, Kathleen. *History of the Chagga People of Kilimanjaro.* The Hague, Netherlands: Mouton & Co., 1964.

Stein, Conrad. *Enchantment of the World, KENYA.* Chicago, IL: Childrens Press, 1985.

Wielochowski, A. L. *Kilimanjaro - Map and Guide.* Nairobi, Kenya: West Col Productions, 1990.

Index

Acclimatization, 94, 116, 139
Arusha, 70

Bantu, 47
Baboon, 169, 182
Bass, Dick, 34
Boma, 170
Breithorn, 28

Canyon, Grand, 19
Carnivore, 191
Cave, Hans Meyer, 15, 137
Chagga, 47
Cheetah, 187
Colobus monkeys, 104
Comet, 20
Coriolis force, 59
Crampons, 19
Crocodile, 185

Dante, 24
Davanu, 69
Denali, 76
Diamox, 118

Ear lobe, 73, 176

Everest, 22, 178

Fairview Hotel, 66
Full moon, 45

Gaiters, 134
Giant Senecio, 113
Gillman, C., 49
Gillman's Point, 43, 142
Gloves, 135
Gortex, 134
Great Rift Valley, 169

Headache, 16, 32
Hemingway, Ernest, 17, 33
Hippopotamus, 183
Hornlihutte, 28
Horombo Camp, 43, 113

Johannesburg, 57
Johannes Notch, 57

Keekorok Lodge, 181
Kenya, 31, 182
Kibo, 46, 122, 153

Kibo hut, 93, 126
Kilauea Volcano, 99

Leg Blaster, 36, 148
Leopard, 174, 179
Lion, 172, 180

Nairobi, 64, 190
Namanga, 72
Naulu Trail, 99

Machame trail, 44
Malaria, 32
Mandara, 53
Mandara hut, 101
Marangu, 43
Marangu trail, 43, 93
Masai, 71, 170
Masai Mara, 168
Masai warrior, 176, 189
Matterhorn, 27
Mauna Kea, 34, 99
Maundi Crater, 109
Mawenzi, 124
Meru, Mount, 60
Meyer, Hans, 49, 92
Moshi, 69, 165
Mtui, Fred, 87
Mtui, Johnathan, 92
Mweka, 43

Olduvai Gorge, 169
Oxygen, 16, 139

Pico de Orizaba, 25
Polypropylene, 134
Popocatepetl, 24
Puff adder, 186
Puuoo Cone, 99

Rebman, Johannes, 52
Reusch Crater, 50, 153
Rungu, 176

Saddle, 122
Scree, 17, 61, 138
Shira, 45
Shuka, 73, 176
Springland, 79, 164

Tanzania, 31, 151
Tlamaca, 24
Trail, Bright Angel, 19
Training, 35, 148
Trance, 16, 138

Umbwe, 44
Uhuru Peak, 44, 90, 145
Ultra-violet rays, 111
USGS, 48

Vaccination, 31

Visa, 31
Vulture, 180

Whitney, Mount, 22, 141
Wildebeest, 171, 181
Willpower, 16

Zainab, 78, 86
Zara, 78
Zebra, 171
Zermatt, 27
Zhivago, 143

Order Form

📱 On-line orders: MissionPress@compuserve.com

☎ Telephone orders: (619)792-1841

✉ Postal orders: Mission Press, P. O. Box 9586, Rancho Santa Fe, CA 92067

Please send me _____ copies of

Kilimanjaro Adventure for $15.95 each.	$_____
7.75% Sales Tax (CA only)	$_____
Shipping & Handling*	$_____
Total order	$_____

*Shipping and handling:

$3.95 for the first and $1.95 for each additional book.

Payment:

☐ Check or Money Order (Payable to Mission Press)

☐ VISA, ☐ MasterCard, ☐ AMEX, ☐ Discover

Name:_____

Address:_____

City:_____State:_____Zip:_____

Daytime Telephone:(____)_____

Signature:_____

Card Number:_____

Name on Card:_____Exp. Date:_____